The Secrets of Hypnotic Golf

Play Better Golf in Your Unconscious Mind with Hypnosis and NLP

Andrew Fogg

www.golf-hypnotist.com

The Secrets of Hypnotic Golf

Play Better Golf in Your Unconscious
Mind with Hypnosis and NLP

Andrew Fogg

The Golf Hypnotist

www.golf-hypnotist.com

First Published 2010

ISBN 978-1-4452-6102-7

Copyright © 2010
Andrew Fogg

The moral rights of the author have been asserted. All rights reserved. No part of this publication may be reproduced, stored in a retrieval system or transmitted in any form or by any means, electronic, mechanical or otherwise without the written permission of the Author.

Contents

Techniques for Hypnotic Golf v

Introduction vii

Part 1: The Building Blocks of Hypnotic Golf 1

    Chapter 1: Unconscious Competence in Golf 3

    Chapter 2: Hypnosis and Self-Hypnosis for Golf 9

    Chapter 3: NLP Anchoring for Better Golf 21

    Chapter 4: Enjoying your Golf 29

    Chapter 5: Winning Golf 37

    Chapter 6: The Power of Visualisation for Golf 47

Part 2: The Secrets of Planning and Playing Hypnotic Golf 55

    Chapter 7: Positive Framing on the Golf Course 57

    Chapter 8: Golf in the Zone 65

    Chapter 9: Pre-Shot Routines: Planning your Shot 71

    Chapter 10: Shot Routines: Hitting the Ball 79

    Chapter 11: Post-Shot Routines 85

    Chapter 12: Being "Your Own Virtual Caddie" 91

    Chapter 13: The Secrets of Hypnotic Putting 99

Part 3: On the Course and Between Shots 109

    Chapter 14: State Management in Golf 111

    Chapter 15: Physiology and Between Shots 119

    Chapter 16: Fear of Golfing Failure and Success 127

    Chapter 17: Anger Management in Golf 135

    Chapter 18: Protection from Covert Hypnosis 143

Part 4: The Secrets of Homework for Better Golf 155

Chapter 19: Analysing and Reviewing your Golf 157

Chapter 20: Better Golf with Less Practice 163

Chapter 21: Playing and Practicing Golf in your Mind 173

Chapter 22: Learn from your Golfing Heroes 183

Appendices

Appendix 1: Introduction to Golf Hypnosis? 189

Appendix 2: History of Hypnosis and NLP 197

Appendix 3: "Your Own Virtual Caddy" Transcript 209

About the Author 217

Techniques for Hypnotic Golf

1. Simple Progressive Relaxation 13
2. Finger Breathing 13
3. The Betty Erickson Method 15
4. Five Steps to Anchoring your Resources for Better Golf 23
5. The Circle of Excellence 25
6. Six Steps to Mirroring Your Own Gallery 32
7. Five Quick Steps to a Winning Feeling 41
8. Six Steps for Creating Your Winning Mindset 43
9. Seven Steps to Effective Visualisation and Sensory Recall .. 51
10. The Key Elements of a Pre-Shot Routine? 72
11. Focus on your Hara to Stabilise your Swing 83
12. Use Nick Faldo's Reset Button to Release your Shots 89
13. Homework for Your Own Virtual Caddy 98
14. Six Steps to Swishing away the Yips 106
15. Other ways of Overcoming the Yips 108
16. Seven Steps to Changing your State, Now 113
17. Seven Steps to more Peripheral Awareness 115
18. Five Steps to Focussing your Heart Back into your Chest .. 131
19. Manage your Anger with the Dickens Pattern 136
20. Write down your Best Shots to Remember 158
21. Eight Steps to Practicing Golf in your Dreams 179
22. Seven Steps to Stealing a Golfing Skill 186
23. "Playing" golf with your Heroes 187

Introduction

I got hooked on golf at the age of 18 and, like most beginners, I focussed all my attention on developing my golf swing. I was lucky to start out with a good swing teacher in Colin Christison, who hailed from Blairgowrie and learned his golf on the picturesque Rosemount Course. He instilled many of the basics and taught me to play well enough to get down to 4-handicap in my first year and to play off 2 handicap for the next decade or two. Colin also took me with him to caddy or just watch from inside the ropes when he went to play tournaments. I remember watching him play in the Agfa Tournament at Stoke Poges with the legendary Dave Thomas, one of the UK's foremost golfers in the 1950's and 1960's.

What Colin didn't teach me much about was the mental side of golf. Pros didn't teach that in those days and in many cases their successors still don't now. However, Colin did give me every encouragement and always told me what I was doing well with my swing before suggesting a few small improvements. What a contrast to some of my later coaches who seemed to delight in focussing on what I was doing wrong before giving me a long list of the changes "you have to make…"

Although I had progressed through some really good coaches over the next 25 years and read a library full of golf instruction books, I was still "trying" to develop a consistent swing when I started to hear about golf psychology. I read the first really good book on the subject I could find and read it from cover to cover so many times it fell apart. What's more it seemed to work to some extent when I remembered to follow the instructions. The problem was that the only time it seemed to work with any consistency was on the practice range when I was hitting shots repeatedly without thinking too much about the target and there were no hazards and opponents to think about. It didn't even work there, if I was thinking about any of the numerous swing ideas that my teachers regularly gave me.

On the course, I simply forgot to remember to follow the instructions on every shot, as I was too preoccupied with everything else that was going on and "trying" – that word again – to keep my swing together. This "forgetting to remember" problem seemed to apply, at least for me, to every golf psychology book, video and audio recording I used over the next few years. I'm sure that many of these products would have worked for me if I'd had the author there to remind me to follow the instructions every time I played a shot.

It seems that I'm not the only one to recognise this problem, as a number of golf psychologists have devised drills to help remind you to follow their techniques. One of the most creative involved checking off each hole on your score-card if you remembered to do all the things you planned on that hole. At the end, you count up the number of check marks and that tells you how well you did. The problem is that the inventor acknowledged that checking off just a few holes per round would be a real sign of progress. It didn't sound like he expected me to succeed with it on a regular basis.

So what's my solution? Well it won't surprise you to hear that it involves hypnosis, self-hypnosis and your unconscious golf programming – the Secrets of Hypnotic Golf. That's what this book is all about.

I have grouped the material logically into four parts addressing the building blocks of hypnotic golf; the techniques associated with the short time you actually take in planning and executing your golf shots; the way you manage yourself during the rather longer time you spend on the course between shots; and finally the "homework" aspects of reviewing and practicing your golf both physically and mentally.

To get the most from this book, I suggest you read through the whole book first and then decide on your own sequence of chapters to study and implement to apply the secrets of hypnotic golf to your game.

Part 1

The Building Blocks for Hypnotic Golf

Chapter 1

Unconscious Competence in Golf

"Golf is deceptively simple and endlessly complicated; it satisfies the soul and frustrates the intellect. It is at the same time rewarding and maddening – and it is without a doubt the greatest game mankind has ever invented." – Arnold Palmer

How often have you heard expert golfers and golf experts imploring us to believe that golf is a mental game? Yet only a select band of golfers use any type of formal golf psychology to improve their game. Maybe you're one of that select band of golfers. If not, you may soon become one given your interest in The Secrets of Hypnotic Golf.

If you do work on your mental game, then a recent survey suggests that you're still in a small minority. Sadly, this doesn't surprise me given a recent survey I read. They asked a cross-section of predominantly amateur golfers what one aspect of their golf they would focus on given a choice. Only 12% supported the mental game.

So what about the top-level professionals? Well when people write about them, they focus primarily on the externally visible aspects of the game – their swing technique. Although there's more awareness of golf psychology, the vast majority of golf instruction articles and products are still focussed on the swing. Most of the golf psychology material that does see the light of day seems more appropriately labelled as course management. Now that's another important and often neglected subject.

Didn't Jack Nicklaus talk about the mental game?

Now when I started out in golf in the late 60's I recall hearing Jack Nicklaus talk on TV about golf being 90% in the mind. However, when I eagerly read his first book, The Greatest Game of All published in 1969, I found very little information about golf psychology. In fact, two thirds of the book was biographical and the remaining third was about the golf swing. Maybe that was what the public wanted to hear or what Herbert Warren Wind, his co-writer, wanted to write about. There wasn't any more about golf psychology in Jack's Golf My Way published 5 years later.

And Ben Hogan focussed on the swing

Something similar happened even earlier with Ben Hogan. I got interested in Ben's ideas about 5 years ago, when I bought my Explanar swing trainer. I had a series of lessons with its inventor Luther Blacklock up at Woburn Golf and Country Club. Now Luther is a real advocate of Ben Hogan's swing technique and has published a well thought out instructional DVD called The Lost Fundamentals of Hogan. On it, Luther demonstrates these lost fundamentals, while looking like, swinging like and dressing exactly like the great man.

So what was the contradiction? Well, none from Luther, but an article from another respected author suggesting something very different. Apparently Bob Rotella, one of the golf psychology greats, had interviewed Ben Hogan shortly before his death in 1997 and asked what Hogan's real swing secret was. Hogan told Rotella that the technical secret was something to do with how he cupped his wrist at the top of backswing.

However, Hogan went on to say that the real secret to his starting to win major championships came when he eliminated all swing thoughts from his tournament play and focussed instead on imagination and instinct. I would describe that as trusting his unconscious mind. Hogan added that he only told people about his swing secrets because that's what they wanted to hear about.

What about other top professionals?

So how many other top professionals are being similarly misrepresented in this way? Two that I've played with, a long time ago admittedly, are Tony Jacklin, in a fourball in 1970, and Nick Faldo, in an open amateur competition just before he turned pro. Tony talked a lot about his cocoon of concentration when he won his majors, but most of what I've read about him refers to his swing and his life in general. There's very little said about his mental strength and golf psychology techniques. It was the same with Nick. He was very impressive mentally and no one who saw him winning tournaments and major championships would doubt his mental strength and focus. However, in those days, all the media focus was on his swing change and people were surprised when he appointed a golf psychologist to help with the Ryder Cup team when he was captain.

Even with Tiger Woods – and no I haven't played with him – we hear more about his swing and prodigious length off the tee than his amazing mental resilience, his obvious use of self-hypnosis and the fact that he's had a mind coach from a very early age in Jay Brunza.

Bobby Jones understood what I'm talking about

Most people these days think of Bobby Jones as one of the best swingers of a golf club of all time. Interestingly he was once quoted as saying, *"The golf swing is too complex to be controlled objectively by what you've consciously learned."* He's also said that, *"The more I depended on instincts, the more I kept conscious control out of my mind, the more nearly the shot came off the way I visualised it."*

Now doesn't that sound almost identical to the approach of consciously visualising my shots and then trusting my instinctive unconscious mind to deliver the shot I'd envisaged?

What do I need to know about the Unconscious Mind?

Well, according to one leading neuro-psychologist, *"Your brain operates on a need to know basis and most of the time you don't need to know."* He puts forward the argument that the majority of the work our brains do happens unconsciously and most of the information from our trillions of brain cells never reaches our conscious awareness. If we start to think consciously about things like physically moving our arms, body and legs when we swing a golf club, we'd simply get confused and fail. Now that sounds familiar, doesn't it?

So the simple answer is that there's no way we can consciously control our golf swing and it's far better to move the conscious mind out of the way and trust our unconscious mind to swing the club.

Read about how your unconscious mind can work

When we consciously read the words in this book, we have no idea about how our unconscious mind interprets the dots and squiggles that make up the letters and the words. All most of us "hear" in our conscious mind is our own internal voice reading out the words to us and we naturally assume that those are the words spelled out on the page or screen in front of us. We expect something similar to happen when we read a green on the golf course, without the letters of course. However, we are much more likely to be deceived by the green than by the written word, however difficult either is to read.

So let's have a look at an example of how our unconscious mind helps us out, as you read the next sentence as quickly as you can and see what you think it says.

Now raed tihs snectene aagin slwoly to see waht it auctlay syas hree in balck and wihte. I ssucept taht it may be vrey dfreneift.

If that one's a bit too easy for you, have a go at this really complicated quote from one of my golfing heroes.

"I neevr hit a soht, not eevn in paccirte, whiotut hainvg a sahrp, in-fcous pcirtue of it in my haed. First I see the blal wehre I wnat it to fiinsh, ncie and wihte and siinttg up hgih on the birght geern garss. Tehn the secne qcikluy caeghns and I see the blal ginog tehre – it's ptah, tacejorrty and sahpe, eevn its baehiouvr on ladinng. Tehn tehre is a srot of

Unconscious Competence in Golf

fdae-out and the nxet snece shwos me maikng the knid of sinwg taht will trun the peioruvs pctruies itno raeilty." – Jcak Naciklus

So what's happening here and what does all this have to do with golf? Well, first it suggests that we don't need to have the spelling absolutely correct for our message to be understood. However, we do have to have the right letters in each word and the first and last letters of each word have to be correct. Second, it says that we are unconsciously very good at making a well informed guess about what we are seeing. So why not trust your unconscious mind more on the golf course?

Well, of course you do trust your unconscious to do these kinds of things for you automatically. When you throw a ball to someone, you look at your target and, without you thinking consciously about any precise measurements, your unconscious mind makes the necessary assessment of what you're asking your body to do and simply does it. It can be the same when you hit a putt, if you trust your unconscious mind to do all the necessary calculations for you without you consciously analysing things too much. If on the other hand, you were executing a similar "throw" with a cannon, you'd be wanting to consciously know the exact distance, the wind strength and direction, the temperature and all the other factors you'd need to assess the trajectory, direction and amount of gunpowder you'd need to send the cannon ball to the target.

But what about a full shot, don't you have to calculate the distance precisely before you hit the shot? Well yes you do, especially if the distance can be deceptive, for example with a blind shot. Knowing the distance also helps with choosing the best club to use. However, note that I said the best club. The better golfers can hit the same distance with a wide range of clubs. I remember playing years ago with a group of people who would always look in my bag to see what club I had just hit. I remember totally confusing them one day by hitting every shot I could, from 100 to 220 yards distance, with my 2-Iron. That sure confused them! I also remember that the scores in those special club competitions where you're only allowed to take 3 clubs and a putter always seem to be just as good, if not better, than when people have the full 14 clubs.

Just in case you found the scrambled quotation a bit difficult to read, I've included it at the beginning of Chapter 6, *The Power of Visualisation for Golf*. There's also more information about the different roles of the conscious and unconscious minds in Appendix 1, Introduction to Golf Hypnosis.

Chapter 2

Hypnosis and Self-Hypnosis for Golf

"Now you don't really need to listen to me because your unconscious mind will hear me. You can let your conscious mind wander in any direction it wants to."
– Milton H. Erickson

So what is Golf Hypnosis exactly and why is it one of the Secrets of Hypnotic Golf? Well, in this chapter, I'm briefly describing what I think hypnosis is and how it relates to my interpretation of the roles of our conscious and our unconscious minds. Many people refer to the unconscious as the subconscious and I have no problem with that. I prefer the term unconscious as I prefer thinking about the unconscious and conscious minds as complementary, whereas the term subconscious is suggesting something below and less important.

All hypnosis is doing is to set your conscious mind aside while accessing your stronger and more powerful unconscious mind. And there are lots of ways this happens to you every day. When you're reading a book, for instance, you're actually just looking at ink on a piece of paper. Yet, in your mind's eye, you're seeing all the action the books' describing in bright living colour. Yes, reading a novel is indeed automatically putting you into a light trance state, providing you're interested in the book.

Many people think going into hypnosis to be like switching off their mind or being knocked out. However, if you're "out cold", you wouldn't be hearing anything at all, so that would be pretty pointless. So for most people, being in hypnosis is like being extremely relaxed and calm, but fully aware, in a detached sort of way, about what's going on around you. Although we experience hypnosis naturally every day of our lives, my first experience was on a training course run by Paul McKenna. There were over 400 people in the room and we'd split into groups to practice hypnosis for the first time. The room was very crowded with assistants rushing about helping people. I was comfortably relaxed and wondering if I was really "in" hypnosis when one of the assistants accidentally bumped into me and nearly knocked me right off my chair. I did not react in any way and just thought to myself, "that was odd" and continued to focus my attention on the hypnotist.

So what exactly happens when I'm in Hypnosis?

During an individual hypnosis session and when you listen to hypnotic audio recordings, the hypnotist may ask you to do a number of different, seemingly contradictory, things with your mind. You could be forgiven for thinking "What exactly am I supposed to be listening to and doing?" The simple answer is that you listen to and follow as much or as little as you want to. Remember, it's your conscious mind thinking those thoughts and that's not the part of your mind that the hypnotist is talking to and you're making the changes with.

The experience is very similar with self-hypnosis, except that you take yourself into hypnosis and use your own hypnosis programmes or suggestions. Some people write down their hypnosis programmes or suggestions in advance and then read them out loud before they go into hypnosis. They leave their unconscious mind to remember them after they enter hypnosis. Others take themselves into hypnosis before opening their eyes, while still in hypnosis, and read their programmes and suggestions. I prefer using a third option of recording my hypnosis programmes fully and mixing them with an appropriate instrumental music track before listening to them at my leisure. The end result is very similar to the Golf Hypnosis programmes I sell through my website.

Whether you're working face to face with a hypnotist, listening to a hypnosis recording or using self-hypnosis, I am sure that there will also be times when you'll be thinking *"am I in hypnosis, what am I supposed to be thinking or feeling?"* Again that is your conscious mind thinking that thought and it does not matter what it is thinking right now, just trust that your unconscious mind is absorbing all that you need it to.

There will be times in the sessions and recordings when the hypnotist asks you to imagine things. Imagining things does not have to mean visualising. If the hypnotist asks you to think of a favourite place, you can imagine what it would look, sound, feel, smell and taste like, you don't have to be seeing a picture-perfect cinema version of it in your mind. You can imagine, sense, think or just know it without seeing it or picturing it in every detail. If I asked you to imagine the sound your feet make when you walk across gravel, you know the sound I am talking about and you can imagine it, but you're not necessarily hearing it in your ears. That is all you need to do.

So, hypnosis is not like being unconscious. It is almost like having a heightened awareness. It also requires you to want the change, have an open, positive mind, as best as you can, and allow whatever happens to happen, without trying to grasp at what you think should happen. Just let it happen and look forward to seemingly inexplicable golf improvement and enjoyment.

All Hypnosis is Self-Hypnosis

Hypnosis is not new to you, even if you've never worked with a hypnotist or listened to a hypnosis recording. I am sure that you have experienced natural trance states many times before – in fact I know you have. It may have happened when you have been driving in a car and thought to yourself "how did I get here?" or when you have been reading a thrilling book or watching an exciting film and found yourself completely absorbed and with your heart pounding. Maybe someone came into the room and spoke to you and you were so consciously engrossed that you completely ignored them. What's odd is that, if they subsequently asked you what they had said, you can probably remember it. Your unconscious mind heard what they said, even though your conscious mind was totally occupied.

If you're really lucky, you've experienced a trance state while playing golf – some people describe it as being "in the Zone". For most golfers who experience it once in a while, it manifests itself as a wonderful sense of calm, relaxed confidence. They seem to unconsciously float along without any real thoughts in their heads. Then just as suddenly, the conscious mind gets in on the act and it just seems to fade away as quickly as it started.

So you already have the natural ability to go into hypnosis and most modern hypnotists recognise that they don't actually hypnotise their clients directly, because all hypnosis is self-hypnosis. What happens when you work with a hypnotist is that they lead you into hypnosis and help you to follow them into an amplified, deeper version of self-hypnosis

Let me try Self-Hypnosis now

Although there are many naturally occurring ways by which people go into hypnosis every day, you have to make a conscious decision to take yourself into self-hypnosis for a particular purpose. Now the approach you take depends very much on the circumstances you find yourself in.

One well known lady golf professional takes herself into a light trance before a round by going into the locker room and finding a quiet corner. While just sitting there, she simply relaxes and finds a "peaceful state of nothingness" that she carries on to the golf course. She feels that she can't lose with the feeling of quiet oblivion she experiences.

When you're out on the golf course and wanting to overcome anxiety, then the *Simple Progressive Relaxation* technique below may be ideal. If you have a bit more time and want to go into more of a hypnotic trance out on the course, or anywhere else, then the *Finger Breathing* technique may be more appropriate. And if you're sitting or lying down quietly somewhere and want a much longer and more relaxing experience of hypnosis, then you could use something like the *Betty Erickson* induction below.

Technique: Simple Progressive Relaxation

This is a good technique for controlling your nerves on the golf course or any other place or situation where you experience nerves. In those circumstances you often feel a tension or physical tightness in some part of your body that limits your ability to perform whatever you want to do. This technique involves progressively tensing up that part of your body more and more. Now release the tension completely while continuing focussing on that part and noticing what happens as the tension just flows out. It's often amazing how quickly this happens.

So let's assume that your hands tighten up on the grip of the club when you're nervous. Then just focus hard on your hands and just squeeze a bit harder at the count of one. A bit harder still at two and increasing to a white knuckle grip by the time you count five. Now, as you're continuing to focus on your hands, just release the pressure and notice what happens in your fingers as the tension just seems to flow out of your body. You can do the same thing with any part of your body.

Technique: Finger Breathing

Although *Finger Breathing* is a very relaxing technique that's ideal for use while you're standing or walking out on the golf course, it works very effectively as a hypnotic induction. I recommend it as a very effective hypnotic induction to prepare you for many of the golf psychology techniques included in this book. You can also use this induction to calm and relax yourself at times of stress and anxiety, like taking an exam, meeting the boss, first-tee nerves or standing over an important shot on the golf course.

As you'll soon realise, this *Finger Breathing* technique does need a bit of imagination, but you must already be pretty imaginative if you're reading the Secrets of Hypnotic Golf.

Step 1: Start by finding a peaceful location, it can be in the middle of a crowd or on the golf course, just as long as you can quietly ignore what's going on around you. It doesn't matter if you're standing up or sitting down and you can have your eyes open or closed. What's important is to be as comfortable as you can be wherever you are.

Step 2: Quietly take a few slow deep breaths while noticing how the air you're breathing in is cooling your body and calming your mind and the air you're breathing out is releasing all the tension from your body.

Step 3: Now, this is the bit where you need to use that imagination of yours. As you're inhaling, start imagining that you're breathing the air in through your fingers and noticing how the air seems to cool them.

Step 4: With each subsequent breath in, imagine that cooling feeling slowly spreading up through your hands to your wrists, forearms, upper arms, shoulders, neck and on up to the top of your head; relaxing all the muscles as it goes. And once it gets to the top of your head, let it continue down over your face and into your upper body as you continue breathing in.

Step 5: Once the cooling sensation and relaxation spreads through to your upper body, start noticing how the flow continues on each out-breath down through your lower body and on through your thighs, knees, lower legs and ankles into your feet with each subsequent breath. Learn how each out-breath cools and relaxes the muscles until it finally seems to flow out of your toes leaving a slight tingling sensation there.

Step 6: Now imagine that the cooling and relaxing air flowing out of your toes as you breathe out seems to flow back in through your fingers as you breathe in again. Notice how your breathing just seems to be a steady rotating cycle with the air simply flowing in through your fingers, continuing through your body, exiting through your toes and then back in through your fingers again.

Step 7: Just continue with this cycle of breathing until you're feeling calm and relaxed and ready to tackle whatever golf psychology technique or challenging situation you're undertaking now.

Technique: The Betty Erickson Method

The late Milton H. Erickson was a doctor, psychiatrist and probably the most famous and influential clinical hypnotherapist of the 20th century. He was also modelled extensively by Richard Bandler and John Grinder and they incorporated many of his practical approaches and ideas into their brainchild, NLP – Neuro-Linguistic Programming. Betty Erickson was Milton's wife and she developed a very simple and straightforward method for self-hypnosis using some of these approaches.

Step 1: Start by finding a safe, comfortable and quiet place, where you're going to be free from any interruptions for a while. Make sure that your mobile and any other phones in the room are muted or turned off. Sit or lie down and make yourself comfortable with your legs uncrossed and your hands apart and resting on your legs or beside you.

Step 2: Decide how long you want to be in hypnosis and tell yourself, "I am going into self-hypnosis for 15 minutes" – or as long as you want – and think about what you want from this hypnosis session. Now take a few deep, slow and deliberate breaths. Breathing in and imagining you're inhaling a wonderful sense of relaxation and breathing out and noticing how you're exhaling all the strains and stresses of the day.

Step 3: Looking in front of you, notice three small things that you can see. For example, they could be a door handle, a spot on the wall or the corner of a picture. Now slowly and deliberately name or briefly describe each of the three items, pausing for a moment between each one. Using my example, you might say "I see the handle on the door… I see the spot there on the wall…I see the corner of the picture of my car." If you don't know what the object is, just briefly describing it by saying something like "I see that round, grey thing over there."

Step 4: Next turn your attention to three things you can hear, like the whistling of the wind, the sound of your breathing or the ticking of a clock. Now slowly focus on each sound in turn and describe those three sounds you can hear, pausing between each one as before – "I hear the whistling of the wind…" etc.

Step 5: Now turn your attention to three things you can feel, such as the looseness or tightness of your clothes, your weight on the chair or the bed and the temperature in the room. Now slowly focus on each feeling and describe those three things you're hearing, pausing between each one – "I feel my weight on the chair…" etc.

Step 6: Repeat step 3 for two extra things you can see, then repeat step 4 for two extra things you can hear and step 5 for two extra things you can feel. Then, in the same way repeat steps 3 to 5 for one additional thing for each sense.

Step 7: Now close your eyes and imagine you can see something. It could be anything from a point of light to a beautiful beach and something that interests you or just came to mind. Pause and let a sound come into your imagination or generate one and name it. It could be anything from your ringtone to someone's voice. Next, imagine or simply notice a feeling and name it.

Step 8: Repeat step 6 for two more images, two more sounds and two more feelings. Finally repeat step 6 again for an extra three images, three sounds and three feelings.

Step 9: By this time, it's not unusual to feel a bit dreamy or you may simply find your mind wandering off. In fact, most people don't get this far before they relax into a comfortable hypnotic trance – that's fine. If you're still not there, just continue repeating step 6 for 4 more images, sounds and feelings, then 5 and so on. Some people may think they are asleep, but generally, you will find yourself emerging from hypnosis at the time you specified at the beginning. That confirms that you weren't asleep and that your unconscious mind was doing what you asked it to do.

Golf Hypnosis or Golf Psychology?

In my twenties and thirties, I played off a handicap of 2, albeit inconsistently, and played in many local and national competitions with varying degrees of success. Oh, how I wish I had known about golf psychology, let alone hypnosis, back then. Yes, I do remember reading that Jack Nicklaus, my idol, thought that golf was played 90 percent in the mind and how he never played a shot that he hadn't already seen himself play well. However, nobody seemed to know how you played golf in your mind.

Here in the UK, people like Tony Jacklin talked about being in a "Cocoon" of concentration when they played well. However, I was being coached at the time by Bill Shankland, who was also Tony's mentor and coach, and he didn't know anything about golf psychology. I believe that Tony was just describing what he felt when he was winning the British and US Opens, rather than explaining how he got into his "Cocoon". Tony certainly didn't talk about golf psychology when I played with him in 1970. That was when Bill asked me to stand in for him in a friendly fourball with Tony and two other professionals who'd learned their trade under Bill at Potters Bar.

I started to get interested in golf psychology in the late 90's by reading the books written by people like Timothy Gallwey, Bob Rotella, Fred Shoemaker and later Karl Morris. I tried out all of their golf psychology techniques, recipes and remedies and liked a lot of what I learned. The problem was I struggled to remember to implement their ideas under pressure. I tried to memorise the techniques and wrote them down on notes I kept in my pockets, but I still found that I'd forget to use them at critical moments in every round.

Now I had heard about hypnosis, but I'd been wary of trying it, given my personal experience and discomfort from watching a Stage Hypnosis show. I felt it was definitely not for me. Then someone persuaded me to go on an NLP course, which I didn't at the time expect to include hypnosis. Imagine my surprise when on the third day of the course they introduced hypnosis and I found myself hypnotising people and being hypnotised. Since then, I've trained and worked as a clinical hypnotherapist before focussing my efforts on using and implementing successful golf psychology using hypnosis and NLP.

There's a considerable amount of benefit available to golfers through golf psychology, but the full benefit is unleashed through using golf hypnosis – golf psychology implemented by your unconscious mind using hypnosis. That way, the changes you make with golf psychology become unconscious, instinctive choices rather than something you have to consciously remember.

Who's using Hypnotic Golf?

So who's using hypnosis to improve their golf performance, apart from Tiger Woods and maybe Phil Mickelson? Well, taking first things first, it's difficult to be sure who's using hypnosis, because most people who do use it, don't want to let on. Why's that? Well first, they want to keep the competitive edge that golf hypnosis gives them to themselves. Second, although it's becoming acceptable for a top golfer to admit to using a mind coach, their marketing people are still wary of saying they use golf psychology or, worse still, hypnosis – that's all too "new age". You only have to look at the comments of Angel Cabrera, a real man's man, after he won the Masters, *"Now I don't have a sports psychologist and I don't smoke."*

If a golfer won't tell you he's using hypnosis, then what are the signs to look for to know he or she is? Well let's take Tiger Woods as our first example. I've not heard him say that he uses hypnosis or read anything that confirms that he's admitted it. However, just watch the controlled and methodical series of blinks he makes just before stepping into every shot. If that's not a hypnotic trigger or anchor, I had better hand back my Hypnotherapy Diploma and my NLP certificates. It's clear to me that he's using that trigger to enter self hypnosis once he's decided on the shot he's going to make. The self-hypnosis quietens his conscious self-talk and leaves his unconscious golf programming to execute the shot.

People often ask me about how Tiger balances his obvious temper tantrums with his use of hypnosis. Well, looking back to the 2009 Masters to see what they are talking about, I realised that this may be a part of his anger management technique for releasing a bad shot. It may upset the golfing public and his playing partners, but it doesn't seem to have any long-term effect on him. Although he's clearly in hypnosis while he's hitting the ball, he appears to come out the moment he completes the swing. If it's a good shot, he calmly moves on to the next shot. If it's a bad shot he cusses and again moves on. He's certainly calmed down before he hypnotically plays his next shot, so his bad shot and his temper don't have any lasting effect – on him, at least.

Chapter 3

NLP Anchoring for Better Golf

"We take the very best of what people do, synthesise it down, make it learnable and share it with each other - and that is what the real future of what NLP will be and its gonna stay that way!" – Richard Bandler

Put succinctly, Neuro-Linguistic Programming is the art and science of the study and delivery of excellence. NLP provides the attitude, methodologies and techniques to explore how a top performer in any field does what they do so well. It explores the unconscious mental processes and associated thoughts, images, words and feelings that contribute to success. NLP also uses the power of language to help clients learn these processes and contribute to their own success. You can read more about NLP and it's origins in Appendix 2.

I use NLP extensively in my work as a golf psychologist and golf hypnotist. I often use NLP techniques within hypnosis, to enhance the effectiveness of the technique. However, a lot of my NLP work is done eyes-open and outside of formal trance. Either way, the success of NLP is based on how it works the unconscious and that's the part of the mind I'm addressing with hypnosis as well.

A Round of Golf that Changed my Life

I originally got interested in psychology as a way of achieving more consistency in the important things in my life – with my family, my work and my golf. I could meet with two apparently identical clients and have a good meeting with one and a bad meeting with the other and I couldn't tell why. The same was true of my golf, as my swing didn't seem to change that much, but my score sure did. I remember one weekend when I played three competition rounds of gross 91, 79 and 68 – in similar conditions and on similar courses. I was happy with the 68, that was 5 under my handicap, but should a 2-handicap golfer be scoring 20 over par the same weekend?

The first psychology course I went on was an NLP Practitioner training with Richard Bandler, Paul McKenna and John La Valle. And one of the big things they taught us was Anchoring. In fact, several times each day they got us to build a really strong, positive and resourceful state and anchor it to a squeeze of a finger and thumb. They also taught us that we could reinforce this anchor by repeating the process whenever we felt any of a range of really good feelings like happiness, amusement, confidence, resourcefulness. We were advised to recall a whole series of memories of good times and when we started to feel really good we'd anchor each one individually. If we struggled to find a positive memory, we were encouraged to vividly imagine a future one.

Now, it won't surprise you to hear that many of my resourceful "memories" were from my golfing life, like the time I won the Club Championships at Brookmans Park Golf Club, my round playing golf with Tony Jacklin when he was Open Champion, some of my best shots and rounds at Beaconsfield Golf Club, my hole in one in the Golf Illustrated Junior Vase and other truly wonderful experiences from my life in golf. I added lots of other resourceful memories relating to my family life as well.

The first weekend after the NLP course finished I got the opportunity to put it to use on the golf course in a medal round at The Lambourne Club. I started to use the finger-thumb anchor as I was preparing to play each shot. For the first sixteen holes, I remembered squeezing my thumb and finger before setting up to play every shot and putt. And despite making a few poor swings and putts, it seemed to be working. I still had a few bad shots, but they seemed to end up on the fairway or on the edge of the green and I was unusually consistent with my putting.

NLP Anchoring for Better Golf

After those 16 holes I was on level par and enjoying myself and I wasn't really bothered by dropping a shot on the short 17th. My 8-iron shot had landed on the front edge of the green and spun back into the bunker. I got out to about 10 feet and missed the tricky downhill putt. I still had the resources I needed and I was still in control. I also hit a good drive down the long par four 18th and was faced with a 4-iron to the elevated green.

I was so excited at this point that all I could think about was that, if I could get this close to the flag and hole the putt, I could get back to level par and score better than I had ever scored at Lambourne. Of course, I forgot the finger-thumb anchor, rushed the shot and duffed it about 30 yards short of the green with the pin just over a cavernous bunker.

You can probably guess what happened next. I got really angry with myself and duffed my third shot into the bunker before thinning my fourth shot out of the bunker and over the back of the green. I was fuming and depressed, but as I walked round to my ball behind the green, I remembered the finger-thumb drill. I immediately relaxed and played an exquisite lob over the bank and lipped out to 6 inches. It could have been a lot worse and, despite the double bogey, I still played under my handicap and had my best ever round at Lambourne.

After that round, I just had to find a way to share this experience and explore what else could be achieved with NLP, Hypnosis and other psychology techniques. That game changed and continues to change my life – for the better.

Technique: Five Steps to Anchoring your Resources for Better Golf

These 5 steps will equip you with an easy and quick way you can instantly create a positive and resourceful state every time you hit a shot or a putt. It's especially useful when you're playing a particular shot, hole or course that you're not comfortable with or when you've recently hit a similar shot badly – like when we run up those high scores on just a few holes.

Now the process involves about squeezing a finger and thumb together to anchor the resources. Alternative anchors could be another physical action, like taking the club out of your golf bag, or a special word or a combination of the two. Watch Tiger Woods deliberately blinking just before he starts concentrating on a shot – maybe that's his anchor for something. The main thing is to pick something that's under your control, can be done discretely and is unique and unambiguous. I like the finger and thumb anchor, as it satisfies those criteria and I can use it anywhere I need these resources, not just on the golf course.

Step 1: Choose your own personal anchor or trigger word or phrase. It could be something like "Great Shot", "That's Right" or whatever motivates you. Now spend some time making a list of maybe a dozen extra-special past experiences where you felt really fantastic. The choice is yours and if you're stuck for ideas, here are a few:

- A time when you were really laughing and enjoying yourself – maybe listening to your favourite comedian, watching a film or just experiencing something that really made you laugh.
- Times when you were very pleased with yourself
- A time when you were ecstatically happy
- Special rounds of golf
- Especially good golf shots
- Special holidays
- Any time you felt unusually good, resourceful, happy, etc.
- If you can't find anything, then imagine something you'd like to experience.

Step 2: Whenever you have a spare moment, just as often as you like, pick an appropriate memory from your list and follow these few steps.

1. Relax and create a vivid image of that experience in your mind. It doesn't have to be a clear picture.
2. Now see what you saw there, hear what you heard, feel what you felt internally and externally and, if appropriate, remember any relevant aromas and tastes.

3. Now brighten the image and make it more vivid and colourful. Imagine bringing the image in closer and make it fill the field of vision of your mind's eye.
4. Make the pleasant sounds bolder and brighter and imagine them enveloping you.
5. Heighten the feelings and sensations you're experiencing and really enjoy them.
6. Finally, as you're feeling just wonderful and elated, say your anchor word, look at your middle finger and thumb and squeeze them together. Hold them together until the feelings just start to subside and then release them
7. You should be feeling really good right now.

Step 3: Repeat this experience whenever you have the time and cycle through the items on your list. The more times you do this, the better and more effective the anchor is becoming. The experience may remind you of other experiences to add to your list.

Step 4: Any time you feel good for any reason, maybe after hitting a really good golf shot, or for no reason at all, just squeeze that finger and thumb together. That'll build up your store of resources even more.

Step 5: Now for the best bit. Every time you're preparing to play a shot, take a putt, or play a difficult golf course, just remember to squeeze that finger and thumb together for a few moments and notice how the good and resourceful feelings flood though you. You can do the same whenever you feel challenged in any way.

Technique: The Circle of Excellence

Of course, there are many other types of NLP anchor that you can use for golf and elsewhere in your life. Many of my clients prefer to use an anchoring technique called the *Circle of Excellence* and there are many other personalised techniques in use. Have you noticed how Tiger Woods twirls his club after hitting a good shot? That may well be his anchor for remembering his good shots. If you use a golf glove and take it off between shots, you could make that your anchor for your pre-shot routine. You could see the logo on the glove, hear the sound of the Velcro strap unzipping and feel the glove stretching and smoothing over your fingers as you smell the leather. If, like me, you don't always use a glove, then find something else.

The most important things for a good anchor are the number of times you use it and the combination of really good resources. The more you incorporate all the senses into the anchored memories the better it works. When you fire off the anchor, you see your finger and thumb, you hear yourself say your trigger word and you feel your finger and thumb squeeze together. When you set up your anchor, you recall the good experiences by vividly imagining what you were seeing, what you were hearing and what you were feeling at the time. You can also enhance the process by recalling what you were tasting and smelling at the time.

With the *Circle of Excellence*, you anchor your good feelings to an imaginary circle on the ground so that as you step into the circle you fire of the anchor. One of my non-golfing clients imagines his circle a flexible ring that he can fold up and put in his pocket. Whenever he goes to a difficult meeting he imagines taking that flexible circle out of his pocket and throwing it on the ground in front of the door to the meeting. That way, he steps into the circle as he steps through the door. He also uses his *Circle of Excellence* when he makes a big presentation. He "drops" his circle wherever he's going to stand when he speaks in public. If you're used to be in the spotlight, so to speak, then you could imagine stepping into the spotlight.

Whichever type of anchor you choose, you can set it up in the same way as I described for the finger-thumb anchor above.

Other NLP Techniques

The number of different techniques available to NLP Practitioners is only limited by their experience and imagination. However two techniques that seem to crop up a lot in my work are those using the various Swish Patterns and Timelines.

A story of timelines

Like golf hypnosis, NLP works best when the client unconsciously comes up with their own solution to the problem they want to address. The role of the golf psychologist is to provide an environment in which the client can make the best uses of their existing resources, skills and experience. Even if I think I know the ideal solution to the client's specific problem, their conscious mind would probably analyse it and reject it.

Let me explain what I mean with a client story that has nothing whatever to do with golf. John was enjoying studying Spanish at school and he really wanted to speak the language fluently. Unfortunately, he was convinced that he'd never be able to speak the language fluently and that got in the way of his studies. I accepted his perceived blockage and gradually talked him round to the idea of what it might be like if he could speak Spanish fluently. He suggested that he would certainly need to have lived in a Spanish-speaking country for several months if that was ever going to happen. I asked him to vividly imagine what it would be like to be there in that country and speaking the language fluently. I had no idea where it was or when it was, as I got him to imagine all the details of what he was seeing, hearing, feeling, smelling and tasting. He seemed to be there and living the experience in his mind.

I then helped him into hypnosis and asked him to imagine that he could float out of his body and travel along his timeline to that future time he'd imagined and to float down and observe his future self experiencing that great experience. After he enjoyed that for a while, I asked him to float back above his timeline and travel slowly back to the present time noticing the things he had done and the decisions he had made along the way to achieving his desire to speak Spanish. I also gave him the suggestion that he didn't need to consciously remember any of the things he saw. When he got back to the present, I helped him back out of trance and sent him on his way.

I saw him again two weeks later and when I asked him how his Spanish studies were progressing, he was very upbeat. He told me that a few days after we met, he had suddenly noticed he was thinking in Spanish when studying and that he was well on his way to speaking fluently. He was somewhat surprised at his revelation and initially couldn't work out where the idea had come from, as he knew that I hadn't suggested it. He went on to say that, if I had suggested that as a solution, he would have rejected it out of hand as absurd. If he could do that, he wouldn't have needed my help.

So wasn't his unconscious just amazing. Without the over analytical input from his conscious mind, he found a way of overcoming his problem and implemented it almost instinctively.

Swishing away your problems

The various Swish Patterns are considered by many to be some of the most powerful and effective NLP techniques. They were developed from the work done by Richard Bandler on submodalities and are based on how we represent our memories in terms of our primary modalities of sight, sound, feeling, taste and smell. In simple terms, the more vivid the memory, good or bad, the more powerful the effect it has on us. Many of these submodalities are enshrined in everyday language. We talk about problems being "in our face" or "on top of us". We remember some things with great clarity while other memories are less focussed. We recall hearing dull thumps and sharp sounds.

The fundamental principle of the Swish Patterns is that if we can recall bad experiences with the same submodalities that we remember good ones, they won't feel so bad. I've included an example of a Swish Pattern, *Six Steps to Swishing away the Yips,* in Chapter 13, *The Secrets of Hypnotic Putting.*

Chapter 4

Enjoying your Golf

"He enjoys that perfect peace, that peace beyond all understanding, which comes at its maximum only to the man who has given up golf." – P.G. Wodehouse

Do you enjoy your golf and do the people around you share your enjoyment from golf? I suspect some of you're thinking, "This Golf Hypnotist guy is barmy to ask that question. Doesn't everybody enjoy their golf?" Then again I suspect that when you really think about it, more of you're thinking the opposite.

What about the top professional golfers? These are the men and women who have the sorts of swings we mere golfing mortals dream of having. They also hole a lot more puts than many of us and they have access to the top coaches and golf psychologists whenever they need help. What about financial security? Well, unless they have serious behavioural problems, they have more than enough money stashed away and the prospect of earning and winning more.

So, do the professionals enjoy their golf? Well clearly some do and clearly some don't. Not surprisingly, a picture of a multiple European Order of Merit winner just zoomed into focus in my mind's eye. You know, he's the man who's still not won a major. And no, he doesn't look like he's enjoying himself, whatever he's says to the press. Neither do the people around him! Many of his playing partners seem to cringe and look away, his caddy appears to hide behind the bag and the spectators feel uncomfortable – apart from the ones who enjoy watching his discomfort.

So what about you and your golfing friends? I know that there have been times in the past when I've been very unhappy on the course and I suspect I have impacted the enjoyment of some of my playing partners. Thinking about it, I know I have, because a couple of them have told me about it, in no uncertain terms.

Now I've devoted a huge part of my life to playing and improving my golf over the last 40 years. Even at one round per week, that would be 2,000 rounds or 36,000 holes and it would have taken at least 55,000 hours at 3 hours and 45 minutes per round. And then there's all that practice, lessons, reading books and playing CDs and DVDs. And of course, there's the 19th hole to consider as well. I wonder how much of that time I really enjoyed. At least it's probably more than the person I spoke about earlier!

Why you play

Improving your golf enjoyment has more to do with the golf psychology of addressing the reasons why you play golf at all than with addressing all the things you're trying to fix in your golf swing.

One theme that comes up a lot in my thoughts and in my writing is the idea that one of the main reasons for most people playing golf is the pursuit of enjoyment, both for ourselves and the people we play with. As a golf psychologist, this is also my primary motivation in my working life and it's reflected in my mission, as a hypnotherapist and NLP Master Practitioner, of helping people to do things better and get more enjoyment out of the things they do in life and in golf.

What about the professional golfer pursuing fame and money from golf success? Well, I suspect that the pursuit of enjoyment played an important part for them when they started out and it probably still features high on their list of priorities as a professional. The top 50 players in the world are probably sufficiently well off that money is not their only motivator. Just remember the look on Phil Mickelson's face after that duel with Tiger Woods at the 2009 Masters. The fact that he didn't win didn't seem to outweigh his euphoric enjoyment from responding to the challenge. It's a shame that we don't so often see that clear enjoyment coming from certain other golfers when they aren't playing their best.

All this talk about enjoying golf got me thinking about what specifically we all enjoy about golf. That led me to recall what Timothy Gallwey wrote in *The Inner Game of* Golf about the triangular link between enjoyment, performance and learning – the three main parts of everyone's experience of golf. Although I agree with Gallwey's idea, very few of the clients I work with seem to think about anything but their golfing performance.

In my first meeting with new clients, I tended to ask questions about what they want to achieve from working with me, what their definition of success in golf is and how will they know when they have achieved it. When I first started out as a golf psychologist, I had expected the answers to be about things like enjoyment, confidence, concentration and consistency. Instead, I tend to hear about things like how to stop their slice, get out of bunkers, avoid hitting the ball in the water on a particular hole or avoid three-putting.

More recently, I've expanded my initial questions to include asking new clients about why they play golf and what I can do to help them achieve what they are looking for. This usually provides me with a much more constructive starting point for improving and much more importantly enjoying their golf.

If I look at my own reasons for playing golf when I started at the age of 18, they were relatively sensible. I was looking for a sport that

- I could play, given reasonable health, for the next 50 years or more
- would give me a complete mental break from work
- offered a modest amount of regular exercise
- was challenging and competitive
- allowed me to develop some good friendships
- breaks down social and business barriers
- and, most importantly, would give me something I could enjoy doing.

Given those reasons, why did I spend the next 30 years, until I got into golf psychology, beating my head against the wall of lowering my handicap? Why did I spend all the hours I could spare and more beating balls on the driving range? Why did I spend all that money on golf lessons, books, magazines and practice aids? Why did I have all those days of frustration and anger when I didn't quite play to the level I wanted? The answer to all those questions is "that's why I first got properly interested in golf psychology."

So if you'd like to get more enjoyment from your golf and play better, why not write down your list of the real reasons for why you play golf. Then you can make sure that whatever you strive for in golf will help you to address those reasons you listed. If you're not careful, you'll end up like those married couples who act like they've forgotten why they got married in the first place!

Who do you play for?

If you're not fully enjoying yourself when you play golf, then who are you playing for? Are you playing to impress yourself or are you more concerned about what other people think of your game? Speaking for myself, I'm definitely out there looking forward to enjoying the shots I hit – for me alone. But it wasn't always like that. I can still remember how nervous I was the first time I played in front of a gallery, was paired in competition with a famous golfer or had my name announced over the loudspeaker by the starter at a big amateur event. I was far more conscious of what other people thought about my golf than on enjoying it and the experience of just being there.

Technique: Six Steps to Mirroring Your Own Gallery

If you're at all concerned about what other people on the golf course think of your golf, then here's a great technique for you. It will make you feel like the only person watching you play is you! And it may just make you play better as well.

Let's try it in your imagination for now. I suggest that you read through these instructions before following them, as I'll be asking you to close your eyes when you do. Remember, these words are

Enjoying your Golf

only a guide; it's all in your imagination, so use whatever terms and language that works for you. The words and the concept may seem silly to you, but again, it's all in your imagination, so there's no need to feel embarrassed – no one else will know.

Step 1: Start by finding a safe, comfortable and quiet place to sit or lie down, where you'll be free from any interruptions for a while. Make sure that your mobile and any other phones in the room are muted or simply turned off. Now, if you're familiar with self-hypnosis, then use your preferred technique to take you into a nice relaxing hypnotic trance with a receptive and imaginative mind. Alternatively, you can achieve the same with either the *Finger Breathing* or the *Betty Erickson* self-hypnosis technique included in Chapter 2, *Hypnosis and Self-Hypnosis for Golf*.

Step 2: With your eyes remaining closed, imagine you're standing on the tee, preparing to step into your stance before hitting a good tee shot. You notice that you have your favourite club in your hands and as you look up you imagine a mirror in front of you, over to the side of the tee. And as you look at the mirror for a moment, you're noticing an image of yourself and you see that other you making a perfect shot with your best swing, feeling the swing, hearing the crisp sound of a well hit shot and watching the ball sailing majestically toward your target, and as you're acknowledging the shot, that image of this second you is floating off to the right before taking up position beside the mirror, there to support and encourage you.

Step 3: As the mirror clears, you're noticing a third image of yourself appearing on the mirror, making a perfect shot with your best swing, feeling the ball coming perfectly off the club, hearing the crisp sound of a well hit shot and watching the ball sailing majestically toward your target, and as you're acknowledging the shot sliding off to the left this time and taking up position beside the mirror, there to support and encourage you.

Step 4: You continue imagining new versions of you appearing in the mirror, hitting their shots perfectly, feeling the ball coming perfectly off the club, hearing the crisp sound of a well hit shot and watching the ball sailing majestically toward your target, and then alternately sliding off to the right and then to the left, until all the space on the side of the tee is filled with supporting images of you.

Step 5: And as your other selves settle down to watching, you're now feeling yourself hitting the shot to the best of your ability, feeling the ball coming perfectly off the club, hearing the crisp sound of a well hit shot and watching the ball sailing majestically toward your target, as your other selves are watching and providing the encouragement and acknowledgement of your great shot.

Step 6: Wiggle your fingers a few times, wiggle your toes a bit and open your eyes. Notice the unusual combination of relaxation, energy and confidence you feel, now. And know that whenever you play on the course you can imagine a crowd of supporters, just like you, standing in front of and blocking out the usual suspects.

You can repeat this technique whenever you like. Why not adapt it for other situations where someone's critical gaze hampers your enjoyment.

What's luck got to do with it?

> *"You create your own luck by the way you play. There is no such luck as bad luck. Fate has nothing to do with success or failure, because that is a negative philosophy that indicts one's confidence, and I'll have no part of it."* – Greg Norman

Many of the golfers I meet seem to play golf like they have the weight of the world on their shoulders and that has a significant impact on their enjoyment of this wonderful game. Someone once described it to me as feeling weighed down with many sandbags, like a hot air balloon that's waiting to rise into the air. Although the sandbags are largely of their own making, many of these golfers think that they are weighed down by bad luck.

So what impact does luck have on your game of golf? By that I mean do you treat good luck and bad luck as two sides of the same coin? Statistically, our golfing luck is going to even out over the long term. If you keep tossing a coin, you may get long runs of heads or tails, but I'm sure that deep down we all know that every time there's an equal chance of one or the other. Luck's been a part of golf for a long time and the earliest golfer's defined good luck and bad luck as "Rub of the Green".

So how do you feel if you hit a really good drive down the middle of the fairway only to see it bounce off unexpectedly into a bunker or end up in a divot? Does it make you angry and affect your next shot or even the rest of the round? Did you see Lee Westwood's tee shot on the 72nd hole when he was in contention to win the 2009 Open Championship at Turnberry? He hit it perfectly only to see it roll on and on before veering off into a bunker and leaving him with a seemingly impossible shot to the green. Would your shoulder's "drop"? Would you feel the world was against you? Or would you just treat it as just one of those things and, like Lee Westwood, just accept the new challenge and hit the best possible shot from where the ball lay under the face of the bunker? Wasn't that an amazingly well thought out and executed recovery shot he hit onto the green from there?

I know I'm labouring this point, but how would it affect you, if you had not just one, but a whole series of unlucky breaks in the middle of a round of golf? Would you notice any good breaks along the way? I suspect not. Maybe you'd start to feel like the course was against you or it was just not your day. Either way, you'd probably not be in the right frame of mind to play well and you'd start thinking more about your bad luck than the shot you're about to hit. If you just knuckle down and focus all your attention on playing the next shot, then you're either brain dead or, like Lee Westwood, you're using good golf psychology.

Good luck can have an equally strong positive impact on the golf mind as bad luck can have a negative one. Looking back on my early years of playing golf, long before I knew anything about golf psychology, I now realise my perception of whether I was being lucky or unlucky early in the round had a major effect on my final score for the round. There was a long walk around a lake to the par 3 sixth hole at Brookmans Park, my home club back then, and there was often a long wait on the tee. As a result, there was plenty of time to ponder on how the round was going. If I was around 2 over par after those first five holes and hitting the ball poorly, I felt lucky despite already using up all my shots as a 2 handicap golfer. My ball striking would gradually improve through the round and I'd usually have a really good score. If, on the other hand, I was over par after those same five holes and striking the ball really well, then I'd feel resentful about that bad luck, my swing would deteriorate and I'd have a really terrible score.

If I'd looked at my bad luck objectively back then, accepted it and simply played each shot as it came, it would have only cost me at most 2 or 3 shots in the round not the 10 or 15 shots it often cost me through bad golf psychology. In all probability, it wouldn't have cost me even that, as I'd probably have some good luck elsewhere in the round to compensate.

So how do I just accept my bad luck, I hear you say. Well just about everything I've learned about golf psychology helps and most importantly, it's the ability to have a good post-shot routine supported by golf hypnosis. After you hit any shot or putt, regardless of whether it's a good or bad one, lucky, unlucky or just a normal one, you should learn from it, release it and consign it to the past. It can't hurt you there. If it's a really good shot, then savour the moment and file it away in your mind as a resource for a future time when you need inspiration and confidence.

Would you enjoy your last game ever?

Many of the chapters in this book directly or indirectly address the issue of getting more enjoyment out of your experience of playing golf. In fact, that's one of my main reasons for being a golf psychologist. And if I could focus it all down to one recommendation, I would strongly suggest that you play every shot and every round of golf as if it's the last one you'll ever play. You wouldn't want to not enjoy it, now would you?

Chapter 5

Winning Golf

"Here you are, starting to get afraid of winning the Open. You're leading by 3 strokes with 8 holes to go. You've obviously played well or you wouldn't be in this position. You're still playing well. You're doing something you enjoy, so enjoy it." – Jack Nicklaus

I remember this passage from my golfing "bible", back when I first started playing golf, *The Greatest Game of All, My Life in Golf* by Jack Nicklaus. Talking about his win at the 1967 US Open at Baltusrol, Jack described how he panicked after bogeying the tenth hole in the final round. He calmed himself down by saying the words above to himself before going on to win in a US Open record score.

When we're scoring well, it's easy to forget Jack's simple message and start playing defensively rather than building on our golf confidence. You see it all the time watching those top professionals who aren't used to winning yet.

Do you play to win?

What about when you're having a great round, playing confident golf and you only need a few pars to play under your handicap? Some of my best rounds came when I started scoring badly and just persevered. The farther I got into the round, the better I found myself scoring. What's more, I got into the habit of playing better and better. Sometimes, the improvement grew over the space of several rounds.

The Secrets of Hypnotic Golf

When I think about this kind of phenomena, a couple of my early golfing experiences quickly spring to mind. Part way through my first year of golf, I had got my handicap down to 7 and I was playing in one of the club competitions at Brookmans Park Golf Club. Well, I started this particular round terribly and it only slowly got better. Starting from the tenth hole, I reached the turn in 48 shots, 13 over par! But by that time, my golf was improving and I was hitting the ball a long way. I started my second nine with two pars then had a run of eagle, par, eagle and I was now flying. I parred the par 3 sixth hole, before eagling the par 5 seventh and parring the eighth. I was on such a high that I really went for the par 3 ninth and birdied it to be back in 29, 7 under par and nineteen shots better than my first nine. I even had my handicap cut on my way to ending that first year playing off 4.

A few years later and I was playing in an open amateur event, the King George V Cup at Porter's Park in Hertfordshire. Again I started badly and although I got better as the morning wore on, I scored 91, 20 over par and pretty terrible for a 2-handicapper. The improvement continued through the afternoon and I scored 79 – still not good, but getting better. The next day, I played in the Senior Trophy at Brookmans Park, my home club, and my golf got better and better resulting in a winning score of gross 68, 3 under par and 5 under my handicap.

So what's there to learn from these examples? Well, unlike Jack Nicklaus in the story above, at no time in any of these rounds did I have the luxury of defending a good score. I was just focussed on my ever improving game. I have many other examples where the opposite happened and I got off to a good start, began thinking about my score and then got defensive. I generally went home unhappy on those days despite playing well.

When winning seems easier than losing & you still lose

Well, it seems that I'm not alone in experiencing difficulty winning from the front and when winning seems easier than losing. While writing this book I was thinking with some sadness about how miserable and negative Sergio Garcia looked even before he dropped out of the running for the 2009 Wyndham Championship at Greensboro. He looked relieved after completing his round, like he felt so miserable that he didn't really want to win.

So what makes one person a winner on any given day and someone else a loser. One thing that rapidly emerged was that it didn't necessarily have that much to do with the individual players golf swing. To win on the PGA Tour and especially to win a major championship, you have to be a good golfer technically. Now that doesn't mean that you have to have a text-book swing. Any method that produces good shots consistently and holds up under pressure will do just nicely. You only have to think of some of the less than orthodox major winners, like Lee Trevino, Raymond Floyd, Jim Furyk and John Daly. Even the greats like Seve Ballesteros, Arnold Palmer and Jack Nicklaus were considered unorthodox in their day. Just imagine what the golf swing gurus of today would make of an unknown golfer swinging like these players.

While the difference between the winner and the man who comes last in a PGA Tour event may sometimes be physical, the real difference has to be in the mind game and their conscious or unconscious application of golf psychology. Remember that YE Yang was number 110 in the world golf rankings at the time he beat Tiger in the 2009 US PGA Championship, but no one would say he generally has the better swing or putting stroke.

If you're still not convinced, then consider this question. How often have you played a stroke-play round with an opponent who seems to be hitting the ball and putting consistently worse than you, only to find, when you add up the scores at the end of the round, that he's beaten you by a wide margin? It happened a lot to me in my early years playing in open amateur competitions. One of the best examples was over 30 years ago, playing off 2-handicap, when I was paired with a complete stranger in the Hertfordshire Stag at Moor Park, the premier open amateur competition in the county. I struck the ball much better than he did on every shot and he commented on it, but when we added up the scores at the end of each round, I was a couple of shots over par and he was 3 or 4 shots under par! I later found out more about Nick Faldo, my mystery playing partner, when he turned professional a couple of months later – the rest is history, as they say.

So the real difference between winning and losing at the top level is more often than not in the golf mind of the players. Sometimes, it's not so obvious until you add up the scores and other times it's staring us in the face, like my experience with Nick Faldo. I seem to remember Greg Norman having the same experience with Nick in the Masters back in 1986. And how many times did Greg fall away in majors when winning seemed easier than losing. Greg's not alone. Think about the number of times Phil Mickelson and Padraig Harrington came second before winning major championships. If all that doesn't convince you, then think about Tom Watson's final putt on the 72nd green at Turnberry in the 2009 Open Championship or what Cristie Kerr described as her "hacker putt" on the 16th green in the final round that probably cost her winning the US Women's Open in the same year.

Your conscious thoughts drive your unconscious actions

One of the fundamentals of modern psychology is the idea that whatever we consciously think about our unconscious mind does its best to deliver. This manifests itself in many ways and if we're consciously looking at something, then pretty soon we find ourselves physically heading toward it.

Have you ever noticed, when you're driving along in your car on a wide road, maybe a motorway or freeway, and you notice something interesting off in the distance to the right or left, that you suddenly find yourself unconsciously steering toward it? That happens on the golf course if you focus on something that you want to avoid, like a bunker or a water hazard? Have you noticed how you tend to unconsciously hit the ball directly at the thing you're trying consciously to avoid?

Well, something similar happens if you're not in the right state of mind when you do something that matters to you. If you're in a good mood or state of mind when you're playing golf, then you unconsciously tend to play positively, enjoy the game and probably score well. If, like Sergio at the 2009 Wyndham Championship, doubts creep in about your ability to win, then you unconsciously play negatively, get frustrated with your game and score badly. If you have natural talent, like Sergio, and if you really focus on a positive result, like he did with his amazing last-ditch effort from the bunker on the last hole, you can still hit some good shots in the middle of a bad round.

So what can I do if I'm feeling in a negative state of mind about winning, I hear you ask? Now that depends on why you're in a negative state and addressing that question would be a good start. But what if I'm in a really bad state and I just can't get out of it? Well try this example of guided visualisation.

Technique: Five Quick Steps to a Winning Feeling

Step 1: If you're familiar with a quick technique for taking yourself into self-hypnosis, then use it now. If not, use one of the techniques in Chapter 2, *Hypnosis and Self-Hypnosis for Golf*.

Step 2: Simply remember a time in the past when you're playing golf really well, enjoying yourself, feeling really good and scoring as well as you know you can now. If you can't remember a time, just imagine one.

Step 3: See what you saw when you're playing well, imagine the scene like you're seeing it through your own eyes. Make the picture bright, bold and active. See all the colour and movement in the picture and amplify it.

Step 4: Hear the sounds that you're hearing there, perhaps the sound of the wind or the other golfers on the course or the sounds of birds. Notice any particular aromas, perhaps the scent of the freshly cut grass or the smell of your favourite food wafting across the course from the clubhouse.

Step 5: Remember or imagine the physical feelings of warmth or coolness in your body, the weight of your shoes on the ground and, most importantly those good feelings associated with this experience.

Feels good, doesn't it? You're playing golf really well when you feel this good, now aren't you?

Winning by feeding off the negativity of your competitors

How often do you hear your playing partners and other people at the golf course complaining about things beyond their control? Maybe you do it a bit yourself. I know I have from time to time, especially in the past. You know the sort of thing I mean. More importantly, have you ever thought about the golf psychology impact that this has on their game?

Now I'm talking here about a whole range of complaints. You'll hear some people whingeing about the conditions. Maybe it's too hot or too cold for them to play well. Perhaps the wind is too strong, in the wrong direction or, as Tiger Woods experienced in losing to YE Yang at the 2009 US PGA Championships at Hazeltine, it's swirling too unpredictably. Some may be saying that the greens are too fast or too slow for them to putt well on or too hard or receptive for their style of play. Yet more may be complaining about the length of the course, the thickness of the rough, the width of the fairways or the size of the greens. And it doesn't matter that it's the same for everyone, most of them can find something to complain or worry about.

The complaining doesn't stop with the conditions. How often have you heard golfers talking before a tournament and commenting on how they don't like this particular course and always play it badly, how they don't play well at this time of year or how they'd rather be paired with someone else? Sometimes, they'll talk about a particular competitor who always plays well here and they can never beat. You only have to think about all those PGA Tour Professionals who started out playing for second place as they just knew they couldn't beat Tiger, as *"he's on another planet"*.

So what does it matter if I complain a little before I play? Well, as I've said many times, whatever you consciously think about, you unconsciously do your best to achieve. You may remember me talking about how if you focus your conscious thoughts on not going into a particular bunker or water hazard, you so often hit the ball straight into or at it. The same thing applies to the things you complain about. If you go out to play thinking consciously about how much you don't like the course, the conditions or your opponent, then your unconscious mind will fulfil your expectations and you will rarely play well.

Jack Nicklaus had a story for this too. He talked about how he used to assess his chances at tournaments by listening to what his fellow competitors were saying. If he heard a player complaining about the conditions or talking in a negative way about anything, then he'd think to himself, *"There's a guy who won't be in contention"*, and mentally cross them off his list of competitors to watch out for that week.

So the next time you're planning to play a round of golf and you start feeling hard done by about the conditions, your opponents or just a string of bad luck, then remember Jack's comments and turn things round by finding the positives in other people's complaints rather than complaining yourself. The conditions are the same for everyone, your opponents are only human and your luck generally balances out over time. Let them complain while you focus on winning.

Technique: Six Steps for Creating Your Winning Mindset

To finish off this chapter on winning, here's another variation on an NLP timeline technique wrapped up in an enhancing light trance to help you to unconsciously find the changes you need to make to create your winning mindset for golf.

Step 1: Start by finding a safe, comfortable and quiet place to sit or lie down, where you'll be free from any interruptions for a while. Make sure that your mobile and any other phones in the room are muted or simply turned off.

Step 2: Now, if you're familiar with self-hypnosis, then use your preferred technique to take you into a nice relaxing hypnotic trance with a receptive and imaginative mind. Alternatively, you can achieve the same with either the *Finger Breathing* or the *Betty Erickson* self-hypnosis technique included in Chapter 2, *Hypnosis and Self-Hypnosis for Golf.*

Step 3: Now, you're in a relaxed and receptive trance, as you imagine a time in the future when you're winning a golfing event that really matters to you. Maybe it's based on an earlier golfing success of yours, maybe it's just imaginary or maybe it's a combination of both. Now imagine that winning scenario as if you're seeing it through your own eyes, hearing any sounds through your own ears and feeling whatever's happening through your own feelings. Make the colours bold and bright, make the sounds comfortably loud and make the feelings in your body and mind exciting and intense. It's just like you're there experiencing it now and it feels so good, doesn't it?

Step 4: Now I know this is going to sound a bit odd, but just imagine it's as if you can just float out of your body now and see the future laid out in front of you stretching into the future, as an imaginary time-line. Notice that, some way in the distance down that line, you know when and where, you can see a future time when you're having this winning experience. Now imagine that you can float forward until you're hovering over that event and float down into it. Now seeing, as if through your own senses, what you saw, hearing what you heard and feeling what you're feeling now.

Step 5: Stay in that imagined memory until you're feeling really wonderful about your winning performance and gather up all the resources available here in this future memory. When you're ready, just float back up above your timeline and float back to the present time, taking just as much time as you need to unconsciously see how you progressed to your future winning success. Notice the key events and decisions along the way. And don't forget that your conscious mind doesn't need to remember any of this, as you're unconscious now knows how to get you there.

Step 6: When you get back to the present time, just imagine floating back into your body before thanking your unconscious mind for this wonderful learning experience. Now open your eyes, wiggle your toes and take a few slow deep breaths as you get everything back into its correct perspective in the present time and place. Notice how good you feel now and that certain sense of anticipation for the success to come.

You can repeat this exercise as often as you like and for a variety of winning situations. It doesn't matter that you may not be consciously aware of any changes that will start to take place in your golf, as you'll unconsciously adopt a new winning golf psychology strategy.

Chapter 6

The Power of Visualisation for Golf

"I never hit a shot, not even in practice, without having a sharp, in-focus picture of it in my head. First I see the ball where I want it to finish, nice and white and sitting up high on the bright green grass. Then the scene quickly changes and I see the ball going there – it's path, trajectory and shape, even its behaviour on landing. Then there is a sort of fade-out and the next scene shows me making the kind of swing that will turn the previous images into reality." – Jack Nicklaus

As a golf psychologist working with my client's unconscious and conscious minds, I find myself regularly asking them to visualise this or imagine that and I often tag on the expression "in your mind's eye". Now some of them "see" exactly what I'm saying and others just look at me blankly. What if I continue and ask them to visualise the shot they are about to hit or to picture a time in the future when they are playing golf really well? Then many of them will apologise and say, *"I'm sorry, but I can't see any pictures in my head, even if I close my eyes."*

However, if I ask them what colour their front door is and which side is the handle, they give me the answer straight away without thinking. It's even more "graphic" if I ask them to relax and to tell me about the best shot they hit in a recent round of golf. They can describe the layout of the hole, the shape, size and colour of the bunker they hit over, the look on their friend's faces when they hit the shot and even the arc of the ball against the sky. But still they say they can't make pictures in their head!

I worked with a client who had big problems with what he described as the "Pitching Yips". His putting and chipping were fine, but quite often he would make a really disjointed swing, usually on a 50-60 yard pitch shot, and he'd either thin it over the green or duff it just a few yards. He never knew when it was going to happen. I decided to help him using a variation of the swish pattern I describe for the putting Yips in Chapter 13, *The Secrets of Hypnotic Putting*, so I needed him to visualise himself hitting a good pitch shot. It could have been when he'd played or just one he could imagine playing, but he just couldn't do it.

Now, I remembered him talking about how well he played the day before, so asked him to talk me through that round. As he was telling me about his scores on various holes, I asked him if he'd played any mid-range pitch shots in the round and, if he had, did any of them go well. *"Oh yes"*, he said, *"I hit a really good pitch into the 15th green."* I asked him what was special about it and he told me excitedly how he had managed to pitch the ball just over the large bunker on the right of the green. He'd had to play that shot, because he'd hit the previous shot to the right as well, so he had to come in over that bunker.

Now, I don't know if you've realised it, but by now, he's describing the hole in great detail visually. He quickly and easily answered more of my questions about this shot, including the lie of his ball, the way it ran after it landed, what his playing partners said about it and his feelings at the time. Incidentally, he described how good he felt when he hit the shot and it was very clear that he was just as elated now, as he told me about it.

He was clearly visualising the experience well and I had what I needed for the swish pattern, so I chose that moment to ask him, in a mock cynical way, if he was still sure he couldn't visualise things. With that clear and vivid mental picture to use, the swish pattern worked really well.

The Power of Visualisation for Golf

Now I know that this seems a bit cruel, making fun of my clients like that. In fact, it's probably better described it as masochistic, because I used to have the same problem myself. When I went on my first NLP course, I really struggled with all the visualising I was asked to do until I understood more about representational systems.

So why does visualisation matter for better golf? Well just look at that quote above from Jack Nicklaus and bear in mind that Jack's not alone in this. Tiger Woods and many other top flight golfers are doing more or less the same thing on every shot.

Visualisation isn't just about what you see

If I asked you to vividly remember eating your favourite food, I'm sure that you'd do more than visualise what it looks like on the plate. You'd probably start to notice the aroma, the feel, taste and texture of the food in your mouth. You might recall the places where you eat this particular food and recall the physical environment, the people you meet there and the sounds in the background. So visualisation is not just about seeing things in your mind's eye, it's also hearing, feeling, tasting and smelling them.

Have you noticed how many couples have a favourite musical memory – they may call it "our song". It usually marks some special event in their lives together and whenever they hear it, they feel as if they are transported back to that event. They tend to recall the scene in all their senses, hearing the things they heard, seeing the things they saw, smelling and tasting the things they remember and, most importantly feeling the way they felt. It can work the same way with notable negative experiences as well.

So, people experience themselves and the world they live in through the five senses or representational systems – seeing, hearing, feeling, smelling and tasting. These senses or representational systems are also the way that people encode, organise, store and derive the meaning of things that come into their brain from the outside world.

The brain translates these sensory inputs into the corresponding sensory representations or maps that create a likeness or a synthesis of our original perceptions. They create our own personal map of reality that we store in our brain in the same way that a mapmaker creates a simplified representation of the physical territory described. As Richard Bandler says, *"the map is not the territory"*. That's one of the precepts of his creation, NLP or Neuro-Linguistic Programming.

In encoding this information in our brains, we don't just use the five sensory modalities or representational systems. We also break them down into smaller discreet units, Bandler refers to them as submodalities, and we store our experiences at this more detailed level. For example, when we hear a sound, we can identify and store by the submodalities of volume, tone, tempo, pitch, pace, direction, intensity, duration, etc. Our unconscious mind uses similar submodalities for images, feelings, tastes and smells. These submodalities are very useful in many other areas of NLP and hypnosis.

As we go through life, we use all our representational systems, all the time. However, we do tend to have an individual preferred system or modality. You will notice that when some people are describing things they often use visual terms, like "I can picture what you're feeling", "I examined it" or "I can't quite see what you're talking about." Other people will prefer auditory terms like "I hear what you say" or "that sounds about right". Others again may use kinaesthetic or feeling terms like "well I feel what you're saying is right" or "I have a hunch that you're correct." Less often, you will find people who prefer to use terminology relating to smell and taste.

There are some other clues to representational system preference available from a person's manner and physiology. Visual people often speak quickly and in a higher than average pitched voice. They also seem to think more quickly. They will appear neat and tidy and sit or stand erect with their eyes pointing slightly upward. They tend to take shallow breaths from the top of their lungs.

Auditory people speak in more resonant tones at a medium pitch and their voice may sound more rhythmic or musical. They often seem to like talking and listening to music. They are easily distracted by noise. Sometimes, they will hold their head on one side in conversation, as if on the phone. They tend to move their eyes sideways when accessing their thoughts and breathe from their diaphragm or middle of their chest.

Kinaesthetic or feeling people tend to look down to their right when accessing memories and breathe from the stomach. They often have a deep voice and talk fairly slowly with deliberate phrasing of their words. They seem to think more slowly than other people and they respond more to touch and feeling.

If you communicate with people using their preferred representational system and predicates, you will much more rapidly develop understanding with them and build rapport than if you cross-communicate. Indeed, when communicating with a large group of people, such as in a presentation or report, it is better to mix up your own representational systems so as to make sure that you hit the button for all the people in your audience, rather than just the ones that are on the same wavelength as you.

It is very easy, with practice, to identify somebody's preferred or lead representational system. Just get them talking about something that really matters to them and you'll soon pick up the representational system predicates they use.

Technique: Seven Steps to Effective Visualisation & Sensory Recall

Improving your ability to visualise is probably more about recognising what you already see and experience "in your mind's eye" than about special tricks or techniques. Most people can use language to describe something that really matters to them whether it's the love of their life, their house, a favourite car, golf course or something wonderful that happened to them. Like many of my clients, I'm sure that you could describe a really good golf shot you hit last week. I'm sure that anyone who's had a hole in one can describe every aspect of the shot in terms of what they saw, felt and heard.

So one way to improve your visualisation is to just remember these special things, people, places and events in your life and describe them out loud to yourself as follows. Even better, describe them in the same amount of detail to someone else. That's what I get my clients to do when they are working with me.

Step 1: Start by finding a safe, comfortable and quiet place to sit, where you're going to be free from any interruptions for a while. Make sure that your mobile and any other phones in the room are muted or turned off. Sit down in a chair and make yourself comfortable with your legs uncrossed and your hands apart and resting on your legs or beside you on the chair.

Step 2: You only need to be in a light trance or just really relaxed for this exercise. So you can use one of the self-hypnosis techniques in Chapter 2, *Hypnosis and Self-Hypnosis for Golf,* or simply just take a few slow deep breaths; breathing in and imagining you're inhaling a wonderful sense of relaxation; and breathing out and noticing how you're exhaling all the stresses and strains of the day.

Step 3: Now, you're in a relaxed and receptive state, just choose one of those things, people, places or events you'd like to recall or imagine and slowly describe it out loud to yourself step by step. Describe the feelings that you had at the time, both how you felt and what you felt internally and externally, in as much detail as possible. Comment on where those feelings came from and where they went and amplify them to enhance the experience you're describing. Notice the temperature at the time and any breeze or other external feeling

Step 4: Continue by describing the things you heard at the time, including external sounds and maybe voices. Relate the things you were saying to yourself at the time. Describe the sounds as you amplify them and make them clearer and crisper. And notice where the sounds and any voices come from.

Step 5: Describe any aromas or tastes linked to the memory. Note where they come from and what they may signify. Amplify them if it suits you.

Step 6: Now describe the visual elements of the scene or the players in it. It doesn't matter if you can't see the scene; just describe it as if you could see it now, all around you. Notice the

The Power of Visualisation for Golf

size, shape, texture and colour of the things you describe and make them brighter and bolder.

Step 7: Repeat this exercise, either in this session or in later sessions, for each of the things, people, places and events you thought of. And when you finish each session, thank your unconscious mind for this wonderful visualisation experience. Now open your eyes, wiggle your toes and take a few slow deep breaths as you get everything back into its corrective perspective in the present time and place. Notice how good you feel now and imagine what you look like sitting here, now.

What if I can't visualise that well?

Although quite a few people initially have difficulty "seeing" their memories clearly, most find it much easier to recall the associated sounds, feelings, tastes and smells. In many cases they are expecting too much too soon. If you really concentrate hard on recalling a picture, you may possibly struggle to see it, like when you try hard to remember a name or long phone number. Have you noticed how when you relax and trust your unconscious mind to find it, the name just seems to pop into your head after a few moments? Something similar happens when you recall a picture. Once you get into a light trance, like when you're telling a story, you seem to start recalling all the visual information, even if you don't actually always see a perfect photographic image.

As with many aspects of life, rehearsal makes perfect, so the more you describe things visually to other people, the better you see the picture yourself. You could describe your round of golf or a particular hole you played well. Use your course planner and scorecard if that helps. You don't have to describe things related to golf; you can describe the layout and contents of your home or getting in your car and driving to the golf course. Start slowly and work with simple objects then expand it.

Alternatively, you could practice standing in front of a mirror, and looking carefully at your nose. Shut your eyes and "see" your nose "in your mind's eye". If the picture is not clear to you, then open your eyes, have another look at your nose and repeat the process. As soon as you have memorized your nose, move to your mouth. Then do the same for your chin, your eyebrows and finally your eyes.

Where do we use Visualisation?

We unconsciously visualise and imagine the things we think about, even if we are not always consciously aware of doing it. As a result we use that capability in almost everything we do in golf hypnosis, NLP and in playing golf.

The power of the imagination and the ability to see things in the "mind's eye" is often very obvious to us as spectators when we see golfers thinking out their most difficult shots. You only have to think of some of those amazing chip shots Sergio Garcia and Jose Maria Olazabal play or the pitch shots of Padraig Harrington and Phil Mickelson, to name but a few. In fact, almost all of the top golfers these days have an amazing capacity for imagining unbelievable recovery shots from the most unlikely positions. In my lifetime, I can't think of any greater exponent of this than the legendary Seve Ballesteros.

Visualisation is also a key part of the pre-shot routines of these players and I suspect that most of them consciously or unconsciously think about it along similar lines to the quote from Jack Nicklaus at the beginning of this chapter. They also carry their visualisation through into their rehearsal or practice swings and hold it in their minds as they hit the ball or roll the putt.

Many of the top players also use their imagination and visualisation skills in their practice. This applies to their practice on the course, the range or the practice putting green. And more and more of them are practicing and playing rounds of mental golf in their spare time.

Part 2

The Secrets of Planning and Playing Hypnotic Golf

Chapter 7

Positive Framing on the Golf Course

"Golf is not and never has been a fair game."
– Jack Nicklaus

When I first studied NLP, I was intrigued with the concept of reframing and the idea that you can change the psychological impact of a problem or situation by thinking different about its content or context. More importantly you can change the way you consciously think about it.

Now, to quote Robert Anton Wilson in his famous book about how the mind works, *Prometheus Rising*, *"What the Thinker thinks, the Prover proves"*. In golf hypnosis terms, this means that whatever we consciously think about we unconsciously make happen. In simple terms, if we consciously think about an ice-cream we unconsciously decide we want one and instinctively begin to taste one. If you're walking along and someone draws your conscious attention to something way off to the right, you may suddenly notice yourself unconsciously veering off in that direction.

Have you ever noticed how if you tell someone to not do something accidentally, that they automatically seem to do it anyway? This is especially true with children, so if you say to a child, "don't spill your milk", then don't be surprised if they to do just that. Contrary to what some believe, children don't do this out of spite, it's just what you made them consciously think about.

Positively reframing the content

You determine the content or meaning of a situation by what you choose to focus on. An electrical power failure can mean that you can't get something done that you just have to do. Alternatively, you can frame it positively to mean you have the opportunity to do something else you'd like to do – perhaps go out and play golf. I had a recurrence of an ankle injury and I was really frustrated and miserable about not being able to play golf. However, I was able to reframe the content of my problem when I realised that not playing golf while my ankle healed meant that I had more time to work on this book.

Positively reframing the context

The context of a situation or event is about where and when it occurs. Any experience, event or behaviour can have different implications depending on factors, like timing and location. We golfers generally dislike playing in the rain, but we're glad when it rains at night and waters the course. I suspect that greenkeepers feel the same way.

Positively framing the context helps a lot with the way you handle the "Rub of the Green" – the bad luck we can all experience from time to time on the golf course. I'm sure you know of someone who thinks of themselves as an unlucky golfer, maybe like an old golfing friend of mine. I'd like to stress that he's not a client and just isn't interested in talking to me about golf psychology – he's still a good friend, though.

Anyway, my friend was thoroughly miserable and moaning again about the condition of the course one day. He also told me how on every shot he just seemed to have a worse lie than he expected. If he was on the edge of the fairway, the ball was nestling against the edge of the rough. If he was in the bunker, it hadn't been raked properly. If he was on the green, there was always a pitch mark just in front of his ball. He just went on and on about his bad luck and how bad he felt about it. And he wished he hadn't played at all that day. I wasn't surprised to hear that he'd scored badly and had neither enjoyed his game of golf nor the company of his golfing friends. I suspect that they hadn't enjoyed his company much either!

Earlier that same day, I'd heard a story about Justin Rose that put my friend's experience into sharp contrast. Now I don't know if you're aware that one of the US golf networks has been experimenting with equipping caddies in PGA tournaments with microphones. The idea is that we can better hear the exchanges between caddie and player. This certainly sounds interesting and could well provide some support for some of the other ideas in this book.

Coming back to the story about Justin Rose, apparently he had been having an "unlucky" day, just missing fairways and greens and bouncing into bunkers – the sort of experience that would have driven many of us, including my friend, to distraction. Anyway here's what Justin was heard to say to his caddie, *"You know, this lie's not at all bad, look at that rough over there that I could have been in, it's much worse."* The whole way round, he turned his perception of bad luck into good luck and got on with the job. Now I don't know if he enjoyed himself, but I do know he scored well that day and I wouldn't mind betting he enjoyed overcoming the "rub of the green". I'm sure that he felt better after his round than my friend did after his. I suspect that his playing partners and the gallery appreciated his positive attitude.

So, the next time you get a bad lie on the golf course or feel that you're having one of those unlucky days, remember to reframe it positively. Think how much worse it could have been and the shot you have to play won't seem so difficult. You may find that you enjoy your golf more as well. And so will your playing partners.

Control what you can and reframe the rest

One of the really special things about playing golf is that you never know what challenge the golf course is going to throw at you on any particular day. And it doesn't matter whether it's a course you've never played or one you've played many times. I've been a member of one golf club for over 30 years and every round there still seems to be a new experience. I'm sure that the top tournament professionals feel the same way when they go back to play St Andrews, Augusta and Pebble Beach again and again.

Now, some of these challenges are to a large extent controllable, even if our golf swing sometimes doesn't seem to be. In most competitive golf, even match-play, our prime concern is to play on our own against the same course. We all use broadly similar equipment and no one else is allowed to interfere with us when we hit the ball. Whether we use a laser rangefinder, a GPS device, a course planner, the advice of a caddie or simply trust our senses, we all have the same opportunity for knowledge of the course we are playing.

What we have less control over is just about everything else. The weather can change frequently throughout the day, so we may play a shot in different circumstances to someone else in the field. However well we play, our opponent may play better on the day. We can hit almost identical shots down the middle of the fairway and one may kick off the fairway, end up in a divot or pick up a lump of mud. The list of things we call "Rub of the Green" is endless and, frustrating though it can be, they are part of what makes golf special. The way we individually handle them is what separates the winners from other excellent strikers of the ball.

You can't control everything

Tiger Woods is one of the best golfers the world has ever known and seems to have developed and honed the ability to control most of the physical aspects of the game of golf. If that wasn't enough, he's also one who's been coached from a young age to have an almost equally impressive mental approach to his game. Between the physical and the mental skills, Up till his marital problems, Tiger seemed to have covered most eventualities, although he does occasionally get caught out by a swirling wind.

At the 91st PGA Championship at Hazeltine in 2009, the wind blew. In fact it swirled in every conceivable direction and Tiger clearly couldn't control it. The TV commentators also contributed to the windy feeling with all their hot air and false hopes for his success. Didn't they just love YE Yang's quote about how the odds

Positive Framing on the Golf Course

against him beating Tiger must be 70 to 1? He based that on Tiger having just won his 70th PGA Tour event the week before, while he had only won his first earlier that year.

Although I've never played Hazeltine personally, I vividly remember Tony Jacklin telling me, and our other two playing partners at Brookmans Park Golf Club, all about Hazeltine's challenges, just a week or so after his US Open win there in 1970. The course certainly seems to have got even tougher, and so much more picturesque, over the years since Dave Hill's scathing comment back then that, *"all it really lacks is 80 acres of corn and a few cows."*

Anyway, there I was watching the golf and really looking forward to the cut and thrust of another battle between Tiger Woods and Padraig Harrington over the weekend with Padraig seemingly putting his demons from Firestone behind him and in the past. I was also hoping to see some heroics from the many contenders from Europe and to see a real return to form from the likes of Ernie Els and Vijay Singh. Given all the excitement, I almost forgot to watch out for all the golf psychology lessons that were blowing across the screen.

Now I don't want to take anything away from YE Yang and his outstanding performance that week. It takes something really special to beat Tiger Woods from 2 shots behind on the final day in a major. It's also worth noting that YE Yang's final 2-under par 70 tied the low score of the day with just 2 other players. Having said all of that, what happened to Tiger?

Well I think I noticed the first real flaw that I've seen in Tiger's amazingly strong mental game. It had been staring me in the face for some time now, especially with his occasional bad results in the Open Championship. The problem is with the parts of golf he can't control and, more importantly, predict. Here at Hazeltine, as so often at Open Championship venues, the players are faced with the uncertainty of a strong, gusting and swirling wind. The wind at the tee is blowing one way, the clouds are moving in another and the flag on the green is fluttering in yet another. Tiger can't predict what will happen to his ball and, unlike his wonderful ball striking, it's out of his control. That's what he doesn't always seem able to handle.

I was taken by the contrast between Tiger's reactions to two particular shots during his last 9 holes on that final Sunday. Both were unlucky and neither resulted from him hitting a bad shot. However, one really seemed to upset him and the other he appeared to accept philosophically. The first shot was a flier hit with a six iron that flew way over the back of the green on one of the many long par 4s. You could tell that he was half expecting it, as he quickly acknowledged what had happened and quietly and confidently played the next shot. His reaction suggested that he'd positively reframed it as just an unlucky shot, not a badly hit one.

The second one was his tee shot on the tough short 17th, where he backed away several times as the wind swirled and changed direction. He looked panicked and more like a rabbit in the headlights than a tiger. Nevertheless, he used his unconscious golf skills and hit what looked, and probably felt, like a really good shot. The ball sailed over the flag and landed no more than a foot too long and nestled down in the rough. A foot shorter and it would probably have spun back close to the hole. Tiger almost collapsed to the ground and still didn't appear to be his normal confident and resourceful self as he chipped out short from a difficult lie and missed the putt. It must be remembered that Tiger didn't capitulate totally and YE Yang hit one of the best shots I've ever seen into the 18th green to close out his victory.

So what do I think was the real difference between those two shots of Tiger's? Well, he seemed to accept the flier as just plain bad luck that could happen to anyone and he just got on with the shot without hesitation – it was out of his control and he accepted it. However, he didn't seem to accept the swirling wind in the same way, hesitated several times and let the result affect him badly. For a golfer with such supreme ball control and the ball on a tee, he didn't seem able to accept the possibility of plain bad luck. He also didn't reframe it like he did the flier.

Positive Framing on the Golf Course

Successful Positive Framing

Well, I seem to have hammered home the negative effect of not framing things positively, so here are a few examples of golfers taking the few moments it takes to positively frame the apparent problems that golf threw at them.

Small temporary greens aren't so bad

For the first seven years of my golfing life, I was a fanatic and played whenever I could, in all weathers and conditions. I was a member at Brookmans Park Golf Club and the course back then was fairly damp in the winter and we were often on temporary greens. I'm pleased to report that they've improved the drainage there over the last 40 years and it's now a good venue all year round.

Now those temporary greens were only about 6 yards across and often frozen. They were difficult to hit and even trickier to chip onto especially after a frost. Although I found the greens frustrating, I soon realised that when we were back on the main greens, my approach shots had become much more accurate and my chipping improved as well. I soon learned to be positive about playing on the temporary greens, because I knew that they helped me improve my game,

It's just one of my six bad shots per round

Now, I'm not sure that I totally agree with this one, but it's still a good story. It seems that Bobby Jones once said that, in a typical round of golf, he'd hit 6 shots that he couldn't improve on, six really bad ones and the rest would be just his normal high standard. I've also heard the same idea attributed to Walter Hagen, Jack Nicklaus and Sam Snead.

Now I don't know if they counted unlucky shots as bad shots, because I'm sure these players didn't hit a full half a dozen of what I'd consider bad shots in any of their rounds. However, it did mean that whenever they did hit a bad shot, they were able to calmly say to themselves something like, "that's alright; it's one of my usual six."

Although I love the positive reframe, I'd rather they'd consciously planned to only hit good shots and learned from and released the inevitable bad ones when they happened. You can read more about this when I talk about post-shot routines in Chapter 11, *Post-Shot Routines*.

My opponent's hole in one looks good on my record

When someone holed in one when playing against me in the semi-final of an important club matchplay competition, I was able to execute a much more rapid reframe. I was a hole up on my opponent on the Par 3 11th tee and feeling confident of going two up after hitting my six iron inside 6 feet. The stuffing and that confidence was knocked out of me when, moments later, my opponent holed his tee shot for an ace. I walked onto the next tee all square and wondering whether I could still win. The thought then passed through my mind that it would be pretty impressive to beat a man who'd holed in one against me. That thought spurred me on to victory. My goodness, I must have been a bit vain and arrogant back then!

The positive thing about being in a divot

Now, I'm sure it won't surprise you that I've saved a brief story about Jack Nicklaus to finish off this chapter. Jack was playing at the Doral Open back in 1975 and ended up with a difficult lie in a divot on the 18th Fairway on the Sunday, needing a par to win. Discussing the lie with his caddy, Nicklaus was reported as saying that the seemingly bad lie would help him to stay down better on the shot. He did and his three-iron landed 20 feet from the hole. Jack holed out for a birdie and the win. Now that's what I call positive framing!

Chapter 8

Golf in the Zone

"When I'm in this state, this cocoon of concentration, I'm living fully in the present, not moving out of it. I'm aware of every half inch of my swing. I'm absolutely engaged, involved in what I'm doing at that particular moment. That's the important thing. That's the difficult state to arrive at. It comes and it goes, and the pure fact that you go out on the first tee of a tournament and say, 'I must concentrate today,' is no good. It won't work. It has to already be there." – Tony Jacklin

I heard Tony Jacklin say those words in an interview after he won the Open Championship at Royal Lytham St. Annes in 1969 and I recall him saying much the same thing when I played with him in 1970, just a few weeks before he won the US Open at Hazeltine. So how come 40 years have passed and most golfers still don't understand much about being in the zone, let alone know how they get into that state of flow.

Years later, when Nick Faldo talked about getting into a trance-like state when playing in major championships, he also called it a "cocoon" of concentration. He went on to describe it as, *"a state of oblivion where I shut out all the people on and off the course."*

Listen to what Arnold Palmer has to say

Some years earlier, Arnold Palmer had a lot more to say about his experience of being in what we now know as the zone. Tournament play, he wrote, *"involves a tautness of mind but not a tension of the body. It has various manifestations. One is the concentration on the shot at hand. The other is the heightened sense of presence and renewal that endures through an entire round or an entire tournament. There is something spiritual, almost spectral about the latter experience. You're involved in the action and vaguely aware of it, but your focus is not on the commotion but on the opportunity ahead. I'd liken it to a sense of reverie – not a dreamlike state, but the somehow insulated state that a great musician achieves in a great performance. He's aware of where he is and what he's doing, but his mind is on the playing of his instrument with an internal sense of tightness – it is not merely mechanical, it is not only spiritual; it is something of both, on a different plane and a more remote one."*

Now, Tony, Nick and Arnie are talking about playing golf in the zone at the level of multiple major championship winners. And they were hitting the ball and putting extremely well for complete rounds and tournaments. However, these players found themselves in the zone even when they weren't on top form. In Chapter 5, *Winning Golf*, when talking about winning golf, I mentioned playing with Nick Faldo when he was playing much worse than I was and at the same time scoring much better. Perhaps he was experiencing being in the zone back then, before he turned professional.

So what does being in the zone feel like for the rest of us mere mortals? Well, I've certainly experienced days when I could hardly hit the ball at all when warming up on the practice ground and then suddenly and without warning, I would find myself totally relaxed and really scoring well when I got out on the course. What was interesting was that I didn't initially hit the ball that well when that happened, but if I missed a fairway, the next shot would be close to the flag, and if I missed the green, I'd get up and down easily. Those good holes seemed to float by and then just as suddenly I'd snap out of it and start dropping shots left and right. I know that I'm not alone in this, as I've seen people playing out of their skins for a few holes then suddenly falling apart, for no obvious reason.

So how do we summarise being in the zone?

To summarise, when golfers who are "in the zone" they seem to be in a psychological state or place where they are simultaneously experiencing

- a calm sense of focus where they are unusually unaffected by the outside influences, noises and irritations that would normally affect them
- a quiet confidence and a feeling of assurance and certainty about their golf
- an instinctive sense of how to play their shots automatically and with effortless power and control
- a feeling of peace, as their normal chattering conscious self-talk quietens and floats off into the distant background
- an intriguing balance of relaxation and energetic action as they swing the club deceptively easily and powerfully
- a sense of detachment, as if they are watching another version of themselves playing golf beyond their normal capabilities and being guided unconsciously by some external intelligence
- a reduced awareness of time and a feeling of there being no past and no future, just a feeling of living in the present moment.

Who else experiences being in the zone

It's not just golfers who experience being in the zone. It's experienced by top performers in most sports, although it tends to be more noticeable in individual sports, like tennis, athletics, target shooting, archery and motor racing. As Arnold Palmer noticed, it also features strongly in the performance arts, like music and especially with improvisational performers. You only have to watch someone playing a complex computer game to notice that the best gamers experience being in the zone. They are so focussed that they are completely unaware of what's going on around them. Outside of sports and games, many religious practices and experiences, especially in the Eastern traditions, seem to involve being in the zone. And it features strongly in many areas of work, especially in the frenetic environments of the stock markets and trading floors of the world.

Doesn't this sound like being in a hypnotic trance

Well, yes it does sound very much like the experience of people in hypnosis. They typically experience almost all of the psychological aspects of being in the zone, including having

- a calm sense of focus where they are unusually protected from the outside influences, noises and irritations that would normally affect them
- a quiet confidence and a feeling of assurance and certainty about what's happening
- an instinctive sense of how to find solutions to problems; automatically and effortlessly
- a feeling of peace, as their normal chattering conscious self-talk quietens and floats off into the distant background
- an intriguing balance of relaxation and energy
- sometimes a sense of detachment, as if they're watching another version of themselves doing things beyond their normal capabilities
- a reduced awareness of time. Most clients think they've been in trance for much less time than they actually have.

I deliberately left out the physical aspects from the list, as I was talking about formal hypnosis, rather than playing golf while using self-hypnosis. You only have to look at golfers like Tiger Woods, who use self-hypnosis as part of their shot routines on every shot, to see how they get the same physical and mental benefits as they get from being in the zone.

Does being in the zone happen naturally?

Of course it does. The similarity of being in the zone and being in formal hypnosis extends to naturally occurring hypnosis. I've spoken earlier about times when you may have been driving in a car and thought to yourself "how did I get here?"; and when you have been reading a thrilling book or watching an exciting film and someone found you completely absorbed and with your heart pounding. Your unconscious mind is driving the car or "living" the experience of the book or film, while your conscious mind is occupied elsewhere. More or less anything that you do instinctively well is happening in the same way – something that you're doing in the zone. That means you're trusting your unconscious to get on with the job.

How long can I stay in the zone?

Well, according to what Arnold Palmer said, he was able to stay in the zone for whole rounds and even whole tournaments. Tony Jacklin and Nick Faldo evidently tried to do the same thing. However, I think that you have to be really focussed and mentally strong to stay in the zone for that length of time. Maybe that's why Nick Faldo sometimes seemed so emotionally drained at the end of a championship. It could be one reason why some up and coming professionals can have a superb round one day and then fail the next day. It can't be technical problems that cause it, because, at that level, their swings don't change enough from one day to the next for that to be the reason.

What about the likes of Tiger Woods and Lee Trevino? They seem to be in the zone only for the time it takes them to plan and play their shots. Between shots, Lee would talk to anyone who'd listen to him and many who wouldn't, while he entertained the galley with jokes. However, he certainly seemed to be in the zone for the few seconds it took him to hit the ball. Tiger's considerably less talkative, but you couldn't lose your temper after a bad shot like he often does and remain in the zone. Again, he's well into the zone from the moment he gets to his ball to the moment he either twirls his club in celebration or beats it in anger.

Apart from the obvious temper issues, Jack Nicklaus in his heyday was very similar to how Tiger Woods was. Jack always appeared to be in the zone as he arrived at his ball and played his shot. That's consistent with his talk about visualisation. Once the ball had gone and as he walked between shots, he seemed to open up a little, as if he was relaxing his concentration, and just stay close to the zone, while not actually in it. From reading his books and listening to a few interviews, he certainly seemed to do a lot of conscious thinking and self-talk between shots and that's not a characteristic of being in the zone. Have a look at the quotation of

Jack's about winning, at the beginning of Chapter 5, *Winning Golf*, if you have doubts about his self-talk.

I think that there's a strong association between what we see when a player's concentrating and when their in the zone. The main difference is that concentration is a product of conscious willpower and being in the zone is more about trusting your unconscious mind when you plan and play each shot. In Chapter 15, *Physiology and Between Shots*, I'll talk more about the difficulty of concentrating consciously for a full round and more importantly I'll talk about what to do when you're not concentrating or in the zone.

How do I get into the zone and stay there?

Well, you could put your trust in luck, just wait for yourself to go into the zone and hope you stay there long enough. More sensibly, you can use golf psychology and hypnosis to get you there when you need to, which is when you're planning each shot and hitting it. So it's more important to develop the ability to get into the zone for every shot, than to stay in it for any length of time.

To do that, you first need to develop a good and consistent set of routines for planning, hitting and releasing your shots and practice them until you execute them unconsciously and instinctively every time you hit a shot. That means getting into the habit of using those routines every time you hit a ball on the course, on the practice ground, on the practice putting green and in your imagination. And your imagination comes in whenever you visualise your shots and rehearse them in your pre-shot routine. It also comes in when you're practicing in your mind, as you'll learn about in Chapter 22, *Learn from your Golfing Heroes*.

Second, you need to remember to do it and that's where hypnosis and NLP come in. Some people prefer to use an NLP anchor to trigger their set of routines and enter the zone, while others prefer to use post-hypnotic suggestions – similar to the ones incorporated into the "Your Own Virtual Caddy" golf hypnosis program.

Chapter 9

Pre-Shot Routines: Planning your Shot

"If I were to pick out one key thing for dealing with pressure, it would be the pre-shot routine – something I work unbelievably hard at. When you're standing on the range with 100 balls in front of you, the more you can practise that pre-shot routine, the more automatic it will become when you're facing a mega-pressure shot out on the course." – Graeme McDowell

Fortunately, there are only three situations in a round of golf where you need to concentrate on your game. In total they take less than 40 seconds to complete for each shot and putt you make. So if you score under 90, you only need to concentrate for at most 60 minutes in a round and less if you score lower. It would be even less if you take into account the much reduced time required for concentrating on short putts.

So what are those 3 situations where you need to concentrate? Well, the good news is that they all happen in sequence. They are your

- **Pre-Shot Routine** – where you consciously concentrate on preparing, planning and rehearsing your shot
- **Shot Routine** – where you unconsciously take your stance, have one final look at the hole and hit the ball instinctively
- **Post-Shot Routine** – where you consciously learn from the shot and either celebrate it or release it to the past where it can't hurt you.

The remaining 2-3 hours of each round is your time on the golf course for relaxation and enjoyment. That's covered in Part 3 of the book

Your Pre-Shot Routine

Every good player has their own personal pre-shot routine and I strongly suggest that you develop your own one and use it consistently for every shot you play. And I do mean every shot. Treat every shot and every putt you play as the most important stroke you're playing in the most significant round of your golf career and use your pre-shot routine every time. Remember that applies to every shot on the course, in competition, in a friendly game, practicing on the driving range and putting green and when you play golf in your imagination.

Technique: The Key Elements of a Pre-Shot Routine

Well, here are the key elements I recommend you include in your pre-shot routines.

As you get the ball, switch into a high level of concentration, peripheral awareness and focus. You use the *Finger Breathing* technique from Chapter 2, *Hypnosis and Self-Hypnosis for Golf*; the NLP finger-thumb anchor or *Circle of Excellence* from Chapter 3, *NLP Anchoring for Better Golf*; or the centring technique in the next chapter and focus on your Hara.

1. Stand a couple of yards behind the ball on the line of your target.
2. Assess the shot you are facing while taking into account things like
   a. your target outcome – where you would ideally like your ball to be when the shot finishes
   b. the lie of the ball
   c. the distance to the target
   d. how the ball will react when it gets there
   e. wind and weather
   f. risks and rewards.
3. Decide on the type of shot you want to play and the club that will deliver it best.

Pre-Shot Routines: Planning your Shot

4. Visualise the shot you've decided to play, see yourself hitting it and follow the ball as it flies and/or rolls to your intended target, in the way you planned it.
5. When you're happy that's the shot you want to play, make a full rehearsal swing, just as you visualised, and "watch" the ball follow your planned path to your target. "See" the ball react as you planned before finishing where you imagined it. Repeat the rehearsal swing until it feels right.
6. Now quickly and smoothly step forward into your shot routine and hit the ball, just as you visualised. Watch it go and then transition to your post-shot routine to learn from the shot and release it to the past.

Using the Right Brain for playing golf

Separating the conscious and unconscious elements of the pre-shot routine from the shot-routine, where you're actually striking the ball, is very important to your hypnotic golf. In an ideal world, you should use your conscious, rational mind, sometimes referred to as your Left Brain, for planning your shots and your unconscious, instinctive mind or Right Brain to manage the execution of each shot. Yes, I know that there's lots of controversy in psychology circles about where these functions actually exist in the brain. However it's actually organised, the conscious and unconscious processes of the brain do seem to work separately to your advantage.

When you learn to do anything new, you employ the amazing analytical power of your conscious mind to work out how to do it. You keep thinking of new solutions and deciding on which is the best for you in a particular situation. The process is very effective in the long term, but very slow and frustrating. It's also quite difficult to achieve, if there are any distractions. This is what's going on when you learn to ride a bike, drive a car or have a golf lesson. Initially, it often seems frustrating or even down right impossible to achieve.

After much trial, error and frustration, you eventually learn the new skill and improve your execution, but you still have to concentrate fully to do it. Then one day, you suddenly realise that you're just executing the new skill instinctively. You've learned the right way to apply the skill and it now seems just instinctive and so much easier than you ever expected. It just seems like you've always been able to do it. You suddenly find you can drive the car or ride the bike without really thinking about it and you can do other things at the same time, like talking to people, enjoying the scenery and thinking consciously about other things.

So what does all this have to do with my pre-shot routine, I hear you say. Well, everything in fact. Every shot you play is a new experience, even if the ball is in exactly the same place as a shot you've played before and the target is in exactly the same place. The grass may be a little longer or shorter, the wind may be different, it may be hotter or cooler and the green may be harder or softer. As a result, you need your conscious, rational mind to plan the shot and evaluate all the possibilities. For me that's the objective of the first part of your pre-shot routine – the planning phase. It's a bit like planning a journey in the car. You think about when and how you want to arrive at your destination, look at the map, check the traffic reports, listen to the weather and consider many other things before you leave the house.

Once you've decided on the shot you're going to play, you should be handing over to your unconscious, instinctive mind to hit the shot and just concentrating consciously on the shot result you're looking for, or on simply nothing at all. Continuing the car journey analogy, once you've planned your journey, you just get into the car and drive, without consciously thinking about how to drive the car. You may be consciously thinking about the journey, but you're still unconsciously driving the car. The same should be happening with your golf swing.

In your golf pre-shot routine, the transition from the conscious planning phase to the unconscious shot-hitting phase is the practice or rehearsal swing. It's a bit like getting into the car, checking the brake's on and the gearbox is in neutral and turning the engine on. If you were flying an airplane, you'd use your pre-flight checklist. Once your practice swing feel's right for the shot, you step into the shot and hit it, without engaging your conscious mind, other than to think about your target result as you drive off.

Pre-Shot Routines: Planning your Shot

Separating your conscious, rational Left Brain thought processes from the unconscious, instinctive Right Brain task of hitting the ball is one of the most important secrets of hypnotic golf.

Pre-shot planning for confidence and performance

When I first started to play golf, I played a few times with my uncle. He had been a scratch player in his youth, but had given up playing golf in his early thirties, due to family and work pressures. My taking up golf had spurred him to start playing again and, although he enjoyed playing his golf again, he was frustrated with his lack of consistency and his consequent higher handicap. If he was hitting the ball off a tee or from a good lie in the fairway, he'd often make a mess of it. However, if he was deep in the rough or had to manoeuvre his ball around an obstacle, he'd almost always hit an amazing shot that would land impossibly close to the target. It was a mystery to me back then.

I experienced something similar with my own golf when I stopped playing so much competitive golf. I didn't notice it myself until one day when I was about to attempt a seemingly impossible shot from deep in the rough and I overheard my fourball partner, one of my regular golfing buddies, say to one of our opponents, *"you're in trouble here, he may not always get the ball close to the flag from the fairway, but when he's in trouble like this he always hits it close."* I knew he was right and that got me thinking. What I soon realised was that I wasn't really doing much planning for the "easy" shots before I hit them, while I was really working hard on planning how I was going to get the ball close from difficult lies and positions.

When you consciously think of something you're planning to do and you know you have the resources and ability to do it well, you naturally start to feel confident about it. Depending on the task, that confidence may relax you or fire you up in anticipation. If you're confident about a meeting you have planned for tomorrow, then you'll probably be relaxed about it going to bed tonight. On the other hand, if you're confident about skydiving, then you'll probably be elated as you're about to jump out of the plane. Either way, you'll be feeling a wonderful sense of confident expectation. And that will almost inevitably lead you to achieve the best performance you can possibly make in the circumstances.

It's the same when you're going through your pre-shot routine and thinking about the shot you're planning to hit. If you've hit shots like that successfully before and you're basing this one on your current capabilities, then you should have the opportunity to know that it's the right shot to play. And that means you can have a wonderful sense of anticipation for the shot.

Focus on your target and trust your unconscious

Have you noticed how when you hit a really good shot, you can't remember what you were consciously thinking about when you hit it? You just trusted your unconscious mind and the shot just seemed to happen. If you were throwing a ball to someone for them to catch, I doubt if you'd start thinking about how you move your arm to throw the ball, you'd just throw it to them – unconsciously. You wouldn't consciously do anything different if the catcher were nearer or farther away or if they held their hand high or low. You'd just throw it toward their hand and that's the target you'd be consciously thinking about.

Many more will be thinking about what they don't want to happen, like don't go in the bunker or don't hit a bad shot. That doesn't work at all well either, because your mind doesn't know how to not think of something. If I say to you, "don't think of a green snowman", you will automatically build an image in your head of a green snowman, whether you like it or not. As a result, you end up consciously thinking about going in the bunker or hitting a bad shot. Now if you remember that your unconscious mind is designed to deliver whatever you're consciously thinking about, then guess what happens. Yes, you got it, the ball probably goes into the bunker or you hit some other bad shot.

A smaller number of golfers will be thinking consciously about a specific target when they hit the ball and if they pick the right sort of target, then they are the ones most likely to hit the shot they planned to. Some very well known golf psychologists suggest that you pick out a directional target, such as a spot on the ground a

Pre-Shot Routines: Planning your Shot

few feet, yards or metres along your line. Others suggest a specific point in the distance to aim at – maybe a building or tree behind your target. Some will even say that you should focus on a specific leaf on the tree or brick in the building.

Now I don't agree with that approach any more than I would agree that someone throwing a ball should target a spot on the ground on the line to the person they are throwing to. It would also seem rather odd to target a tree, a house or something on the wall in the background, now wouldn't it. Once again, you'd target the hand of the person you're throwing to.

So why not simply target the place you want the ball to finish and let your unconscious mind work out how to hit the ball there. Even better, why not think about the route that the ball will take to get there, including the way you expect the ball to fly, bounce and roll. If you're doing the visualisation part of your pre-shot routine correctly, then you've already got the picture you should be thinking about when you hit the ball.

Chapter 10

Shot Routines: Hitting the Ball

"I was becoming too knowledgeable about my own swing, and sometimes knowledge can be a bit of a disadvantage. So I really just tried to quiet my mind down a little bit and get back to playing golf."
– Graeme McDowell

I'm regularly asked by clients about what they should be thinking about in their golf mind when they are actually swinging the club or stroking a putt. Many of them will have some sort of pre-shot routine that prepares them for the shot they are about to make. A smaller number will also include some sort of visualisation of the shot they want to hit. However, very few will be thinking about that visualisation when they actually hit the ball.

So what are they thinking about when they hit the shot? Well, a lot of them are consciously thinking about some aspect of their swing mechanics and that doesn't work at all well. That's because your conscious mind doesn't work fast enough to control your golf swing. So what should you do?

Well, you've used your conscious mind and your pre-shot routine to plan your shot meticulously; you've spent a short time visualising the shot; you've "seen" yourself hitting the ball; and "watched" the ball fly and/or roll to your target as you visualised it would. Finally you physically rehearsed the swing you'd visualised until it felt right.

Now you're ready to use your unconscious shot routine to hit the ball, taking only as much time as you need to keep the feeling of your rehearsal swing and the shot you visualised at the front of your mind, as you swing the club and hit the ball.

Here's what you have to do

You already have the club in your hand and you're still gripping it correctly after the successful rehearsal swing, so all you really have to do is unconsciously

1. step forward to the ball and take your stance
2. glance to double check your body and clubface alignment
3. relax yourself briefly
4. take one last lingering look at your target
5. start your swing as your eyes return to the ball – there's nothing more you can do now, but hit it!

And all you need to think about is stepping into yourself and experiencing the shot you're visualising and have just rehearsed. The rest is just about keeping you conscious mind occupied with that and trusting your unconscious mind to hit the shot you visualised.

It really is that easy and shouldn't take you more than a few seconds.

Streamline your transition from pre-shot to hitting the ball

Golf instructors often talk about the transition in the golf swing as that pause between completing the backswing and starting the downswing. They often suggest that slowing down the transition is one of the most important keys to hitting a good shot.

Although I'm not a swing coach, I am qualified to comment on what for me is an even more important transition in golf psychology. It's the transition from the conscious analytical planning phase of your pre-shot routine to the unconscious instinctive phase of actually hitting the ball. Unlike the pause at the top of the backswing, the faster you can comfortably and smoothly make this transition, the better and more consistently you'll find yourself striking the ball or rolling the putt.

Shot Routines: Hitting the Ball

If you watch the top players in the world, like Phil Mickelson and Tiger Woods, you'll notice that they take very little time between taking their chosen club out of the bag and hitting the ball. A recent study suggested that they consistently take around 11 to 12 seconds to do this and they are very consistent with the timing. If they take any longer, they often hit a less than good shot – these guys don't hit many downright bad shots.

Now just to be clear, that short time includes any practice swings they may take, as well as taking their stance and hitting the ball. What's interesting is that they don't seem at all rushed in fitting everything into such an apparently short time. They certainly don't have any spare time for self doubt and any little voice in their head telling them they are doing it all wrong! In fact, they complete the process like they are in some sort of trance. That suggests that they are leaving the whole process to their unconscious golf minds, just like driving a car or riding a bike.

Now some of the players you watch on TV or out on the course take a lot longer to make this transition and they are less consistent in their timing. How well did you see them play? If you watched Sergio Garcia playing golf a few years ago, you'd have often seen him take an inordinately long time to hit the ball. He had a pained expression on his face that suggested he was experiencing a lot of negative self-talk and he seemed to be wringing the life out of the club as he repeatedly re-gripped his hands. It's no surprise that his golf was inconsistent at best, despite his amazing shot-making ability. He certainly didn't seem to be enjoying his golf.

So how do I speed up my transition from taking the club out of the bag to hitting the ball, I hear you say? Well one way is to make as much of the process as instinctive and unconscious as you can. Streamline your own transition process and use it every time you hit a shot on the golf course, at the driving range, on the practice putting green and in your mental golf practice.

How critical is your clubface alignment?

I've already spoken about the advantages of a quick transition from the final rehearsal swing to actually striking the ball. And one of the areas many golfers seem to take a lot of time over is their club alignment. If like most people, you place the club behind or beside the ball as you take up your stance, it's likely that it's fairly well aligned right from the start.

So how much is the accuracy of your golf shot influenced by club alignment at address and how much is down to your instinctive or unconscious golf ability? Now I'm not talking here about the complexity of aligning the various parts of your body when you practice. That's a subject for your golf pro, not your golf psychologist. All I'm interested in here is the alignment of your club face at address and how accurately you can consciously aim your club face.

Starting with a few technical facts, a typical club head is about 3 inches wide from heel to toe and the hitting area is less than 2 inches wide. With a mid-iron, those two inches sit on the ground about 4-5 feet from your eyes, depending on your height and style. How precise can you be with the alignment of that clubhead from that distance?

If you were an eight of an inch out with the face alignment, then your club would be facing about 10 yards wide of your target 160 yards away – the difference between hitting or missing an average green. Now, I know that the path the club head takes at impact has a different effect on the direction the ball starts flying, than the alignment of the clubface, but that's more than compensated for by any slice or draw swing created and the tendency for us golfers to swing square to our clubface.

So, how do the better golfers maintain their accuracy if it's so difficult to align the clubface accurately? Well, let's look at other sports where the action is so rapid that we don't have time to think consciously about alignment. How often have you seen a top-class cricket fielder throw the ball from maybe 40 yards more than a yard either side of the wicket-keeper? That's despite having to run some way for the ball, pick it up, turn and throw it back as quickly as possible. I suspect that something similar happens in baseball. Now, do they spend any time aligning themselves consciously before they throw the ball? I don't think so. They just turn and throw the ball and trust their amazing bodies and unconscious minds to assess all the variables and let fly.

Shot Routines: Hitting the Ball

The same goes for tennis where there's little or no time for alignment. Timothy Gallwey's original Inner Game book made similar arguments for the capabilities of the unconscious mind in the game of tennis. When he talked about Self 1 and Self 2, he was talking about what I describe as the conscious and unconscious minds. Even with the dynamic nature of tennis, he found a need for a distraction to stop the conscious mind interfering with the shot – calling out "Bounce" and "Hit" when the ball bounced or you hit it with the racket.

Now you know the benefits of shortening your shot-routine, think about taking less time with your club alignment when you're setting up to play your shots and trust your unconscious to hit the shot where you want it to go. Work on it on the practice ground and in your mental practice until it becomes second nature and you know it works well for you. Then take it to the course and enjoy the results.

Technique: Focus on your Hara to Stabilise your Swing

Breathing deeply down into the lower part of your lungs generally relaxes you and this can be enhanced by briefly focusing your attention at a point just below your navel. It's the physical balance point of your body and is known in a number of Eastern philosophies as your Hara. Focussing on this point, albeit briefly, calms, relaxes and physically balances and stabilises you in preparation for taking that last lingering look at your target before you swing the club.

I learned about the Hara on an NLP course run by Richard Bandler and had the opportunity to practice the technique there. I worked on it with a fellow student on the course and got her to just stand in an upright, relaxed posture and then to focus her mind on a point on the far wall. I then gently pushed her sideways with my hand against the outside of her shoulder. It was very easy to cause her to sway off balance with just a slight push.

I then repeated the exercise, but this time asking her to focus all her attention on her Hara and then repeated the push on her shoulder. This time I couldn't budge her, however hard I pushed. I was particularly surprised that the she remained calm and relaxed despite my attempts to shove her off balance. We then repeated the exercise with her pushing me and she achieved the same results

Chapter 11

Post-Shot Routines

"Golf is about how well you accept, respond to, and score with your misses much more so than it is a game of your perfect shots." – Dr Bob Rotella

So you've positively framed any negative issues, you've consciously planned and rehearsed your shot and you've struck the ball. Now what? Don't you just have to replace the divot, smooth the sand or put the flag back in the hole before putting the club back in the bag and moving on to prepare to play the next shot?

Well yes, we all have to have to do all those things or at least make sure that someone does them for us. But there is still a lot more that people do. For example if the shot didn't finish as well as planned, some players

- rant and rave out loud
- physically abuse their club, the course or their equipment
- throw their club – sometimes toward their caddy or into the gallery, if they have one
- are still worrying about the shot when they are hitting the next one
- look for someone or some thing to blame
- start thinking about what's wrong with their swing mechanics
- get down on themselves and call themselves awful names
- trudge forward miserably with their head hanging down while dreading the next shot
- take the memory of the bad shot with them to haunt them.

Interestingly, few if any learn anything from the shot and most unconsciously attach or anchor their bad feelings to the hole, the course, the club they used, the type of shot they hit and to their golf in general.

If the shot did go well, most people react positively and celebrate it to some degree. That's good, because when you react positively after hitting a golf shot, your brain produces lots of happy chemicals and associates those good feelings with the shot you've just hit and to the hole you've just played. The next time you play that hole or play a similar shot, you have the opportunity to unconsciously remember that feeling and the associated result. In NLP terms, this is natural anchoring.

The very best golfers really enjoy their good shots – they want to remember them. And they also release their bad shots to the past without any emotion, like someone else hit that bad shot. You can't physically go back in time and replay a shot, so just forget it and move on.

Now, I'd prefer to leave you to develop your own detailed post-shot routine, as it's most important that you're comfortable with it and make it natural for you. Just think about including these four elements in your post-shot routine.

1. Identify a specific trigger for the start of your post-shot routine, like seeing the ball stop moving.
2. If it's a good shot, then really feel good and replay the shot in your mind just as well as it felt when you hit it or even better.
3. If it's not a shot to remember, then don't react at all and just see it briefly – as if you were watching someone else play the shot.
4. Good or bad, consciously release the shot to the past, where it can't hurt you and relax as you start walking forward to the next shot.

Learn from every shot and every putt

One of the key lessons for success in life, in business and on the golf course is learning from your mistakes. If you're not making mistakes, then you probably aren't testing yourself enough and

Post-Shot Routines

making the full use of your capabilities and resources. The good news for us human beings is that we're programmed from birth with the natural skill for learning by trial and error.

Milton Erickson, the father of modern hypnotherapy, often used the story of how he learned to walk again, at the age of 18 and after almost dying from Polio, by watching his baby sister learning to walk. He describes it in his book *The February Man*.

"When she first learns to walk, she picks up her right foot and moves it one step ahead. And then after that she has had the experience of moving her right foot so she moves the right foot again and takes another step ahead. She doesn't learn to walk all at once, by putting one foot up and then the other, so she learns to walk this way and then she tumbles. But the baby has to learn to do it one foot after another. She makes mistakes in learning to walk, and she learns how with the fewest possible tumbles and without trying to hurry too much."

He goes on to describe how, especially when we are very young, we seem to be programmed for this trial and error style of learning and we gradually piece together our experience of what works. That way we come up with our own personal method for doing things. That's probably how you learned to walk, to tie your shoes, to ride a bike and to drive a car. Hopefully with more trial than error with that last example!

Erickson often used this story as a metaphor for a wide range of learning situations and it applies equally well to our lifetime learning of the wonderful game of golf.

So every time you make a mistake on the golf course and maybe hit a bad shot, learn from it then release it to the graveyard of all the bad shots anyone ever hit. You've taken your learnings from the shot and discarded it. It will never bother you again, unless you dwell on it. You can also use the same technique to learn from other people's successes and failures; whether they are your playing partners or the players you're watching in a tournament.

Ross Fisher must have a pretty good post-shot routine

One up and coming top young British professional is Ross Fisher and there are just so many reasons why he's succeeding so well and must inevitably win more and more. If I had to choose just one reason and one example to illustrate it here, it just has to be his ability to handle the bad and unlucky breaks, like he did during the 2009 Open Championship at Turnberry.

Now, I already thought of Ross Fisher as such a wonderful, personable and polite young golfer, so I was in seventh heaven when he left the 4th green on the Sunday leading the Open by two shots. It was even better that one of my all time favourites Tom Watson was only 2 behind and Lee Westwood, another favourite of mine, was in the mix and also playing at the top of his game. This was going to be a real treat. I was also aware that one of my old clubmates, Luke Donald, was posting a leading score in the clubhouse with a final round 67.

After both Ross and Lee hit their irons off the 5th tee into the rough, I was concerned that they might both drop a shot, but I never dreamt that Ross would drop four! He didn't really do anything wrong on that hole, it was just the "rub of the green" that you can get on a traditional links course. He had a terrible lie in thick grass, had nowhere to drop and when he played it, the ball ended up in an even worse spot. He eventually got out onto the fairway playing six, hit a good shot onto the green and nearly holed a very good approach putt.

It all reminded me of rounds that I've had, playing in top amateur competitions and from the championship tees at Open Championship venues, like Royal Birkdale and Royal St Georges, where the rough could be almost unfairly penalising. What was different about Ross was that he just kept smiling, stuck to his routine and got on with it. He even smiled and doffed his hat in response to the applause from the crowds when he finally holed out for an 8 on that 5th green. What's more, he parred the next hole and his last 10 holes. In other words, he accepted that these things happen on the golf course and just got on with his job as a professional golfer, hitting good shots and pleasing the crowd. And just in case you forgot, he had the impending birth of his first child to think about as well.

At the risk of repeating myself, the next time you're out on the course and the golfing gods or your golf mind seem to be against you, remember how Ross Fisher handled it at that Open Championship. Accept what happened, consign it to the past where it can no longer hurt you and get on with playing the next shot to the best of your ability. And keep smiling and enjoying this wonderful game of golf.

Technique: Use Nick Faldo's Reset Button to Release your Shots

The ability to learn from your bad shots and then release them from your mind is one of the keys to consistent scoring. You only have to look at the world's greatest ever golfers to see this. I don't ever recall seeing the likes of Jack Nicklaus, Tiger Woods and Nick Faldo dwelling for any length of time over a bad shot or allowing one to affect a subsequent shot they had to play. They certainly got over it long before they played their next shot and just carried on with their regular routine.

One of the key techniques in the application of golf hypnosis is the use of metaphor to communicate a concept that may be rejected or over analysed by the conscious mind. As an example, if I wanted someone to swing their golf club naturally and unconsciously, I might talk to them about the way they throw a ball of paper into a wastepaper basket or skim a stone across a pond – without any conscious thought.

So I'm always on the lookout for a good metaphor and I needed one to use in my golf hypnosis to help people with their post-shot routines. In particular, to help them to learn whatever they can from a bad shot and then forget about it and move on, "in the zone" or "in the now", to their next one.

So, imagine my delight when I was listening to Nick Faldo on the television, commentating on the 2009 Tour Championship at East Lake. Tiger Woods had just pushed his tee shot way out to the right and was in the middle of slamming his driver into the ground with a dramatic lunge. Then suddenly he just seemed to switch off, his eyes glazed over like he was in a light hypnotic trance and he calmly bent down, picked up his tee and walked off in the direction of his ball. As he did so, Nick commented about Tiger hitting the "reset button" and getting back "in the now". A very large, if metaphoric, light bulb lit up in my head and I just knew that I had to include that metaphor in my work.

If you're comfortable using self-hypnosis, then why not incorporate Nick's "reset button" or your own metaphor into your hypnotic post-shot routing programme and it'll just happen unconsciously. Alternatively, you could create your own "reset button" with an NLP anchor, like the *Circle of Excellence* technique in Chapter 3 *NLP Anchoring for Better Golf*, that fires off automatically whenever you're in that situation.

Chapter 12

Being "Your Own Virtual Caddy"

"Success depends almost entirely on how effectively you learn to manage the game's two ultimate adversaries: the course and yourself."
– Jack Nicklaus

How many times have you seen a top professional golfer in deep conversation with his or her caddie, when you're watching golf on television? It almost seems like there are two people out there playing as a team – one doing the thinking and one doing the playing.

I was just watching the last few holes of the 2008 Open Championship again on video and marvelling at the battle between Padraig Harrington, Ian Poulter and the amazing Greg Norman – how does he play golf to that standard over 4 days at 53, having hardly hit a ball all year?

Anyway, I'm watching Harrington surveying his shot to the 17th at Royal Birkdale and consulting as usual with Ronan Flood, his caddy and brother-in-law, over his 259 yard second shot into the par 5. The camera zoomed in on their discussion and then suddenly Padraig's eyes seemed to glaze over and, as Ronan gave him some last few words of encouragement, he just seemed to hit the shot as if on autopilot.

Well, we all know what happened. His five-wood travelled straight as a die, landing on the firm fairway and bounding up on to the green before slowing to a halt less than three feet from the hole – absolutely unbelievable!

Padraig's conversations with Ronan continued as they nurtured each other down the final hole and on to a second successive Open title. It was so very different from 2007 when Padraig was quoted as saying, *"You know, Ronan did a hell of a job dragging me back into the 18th after I had hit that second shot into the water and you can see from the pitch and the putt that I was back in the zone"*. So it was a team event that year as well.

Tiger Woods has a similar relationship with his caddy, Steve Williams. Steve was already an experienced caddy when he paired up with Tiger. He worked with Greg Norman, Wayne Grady and Ray Floyd, all major champions before teaming up with Tiger in 1999.

Steve summed up his partnership with Tiger saying, *"I set myself a target that within the first year, 1999, we would have won a tournament – to prove that we had a good chemistry; to win in the States – to prove it was no walkover; and to win a major – the biggest ambition for any player or caddy. Fortunately, we accomplished all three with Tiger's victory at the US PGA that August."*

In that event, with Sergio Garcia on a charge, Woods was just one stroke ahead with an eight-foot putt to maintain that lead. Tiger thought the line on it was outside left, but as Steve later remembered, *"I kept on saying to him: 'No, no, it's inside left. I've seen this before.' He took my advice and in it dropped."* Later that year, Tiger sent him a framed photo of him holding the US PGA trophy and had written on it, "Great read on 17!"

What about the amateur golfer? Well, very few amateurs use caddies at all and those who do don't have the sort of relationship enjoyed by Tiger and Steve or Padraig and Ronan.

The vast majority of amateur golfers are both caddy and golfer, but the caddy part tends to be just a bag carrier or trolley puller. What's more, the caddy part keeps nagging the player part the whole time, even when playing the shot. There's no escape into the Zone. How would Padraig cope if Ronan kept nagging him while he's playing the shot?

Being "Your Own Virtual Caddy"

Caddies like Ronan Flood and Steve Williams spend a lot of time walking the course, noting distances, the best positions for approach shots, the slopes and speed of the greens and a host of other things. Amateurs have a lot of this information too. They have yardage markers, yardage charts, GPS and laser rangefinders. And, of course, they often play the same course every week.

What Ronan and Steve also do is to manage their player. They remind them when to concentrate, when to relax and when to release the shot they've just played – good or bad. They also remind their player about current swing thoughts, pre-shot routines and mental strategies. The amateur has to remember all these things for himself and often doesn't.

A leading Golf Psychologist has even devised a memory game in an attempt to help golfers to remember these things. You mark off the hole-number on your scorecard, if you remember all the golf psychology instructions you wanted to use on that hole. He suggests that successfully marking off 6 out of 18 holes is a good score, so that mean's your mental caddy's gone walkabout for the other 12 holes. Steve and Ronan would get their marching orders if they allowed that to happen. In reality, most people struggle to mark off a single hole without outside help.

So what about my own experience? Well, the only time I ever used a caddy was in my younger days and the caddy was even younger than I was. And he was solely there to carry the bag. However, I did have a playing partner years ago with whom I always played really well. In writing this article I suddenly realised why!

Tom was a friend of my late father. He took up golf in his early 50's and rapidly became a golf fanatic – it often happens, doesn't it. Tom's idol was Arnold Palmer and he even used to refer to himself as "Arnie". His favourite "Arnie" quote was *"If all else fails, I can always dig ditches"*, but in Tom's case, that was the way he played golf!

I was playing off 2-handicap in those days and my father asked me to play regularly with Tom to help him get his handicap down. It was an interesting experience, because Tom always got to my ball before I did and demanded politely that I explain what I was planning to do with the shot. I would describe the shot I was faced with, the distance and club selection, the effect of the wind and the lie, the landing conditions at the target area and which side of the hole I wanted to land the ball. I would go through a similar description for every drive, every shot, every chip and every putt.

The odd thing was that every time I played with Tom, I scored really well, despite my frustration with his golf. The last round I played with him I scored 68, 3-under par and my best-ever medal score. What's odd is that I wasn't striking the ball that well. I could never explain why I played so well with Tom – until now.

With the power of hindsight and with my training in Hypnotherapy and NLP, I now realise that by explaining everything to Tom, I became my own virtual caddy. By the time I actually addressed the ball and swung the club, I had a clear visualisation of the successful shot I wanted to play and all I had to do was let my unconscious mind deliver the shot. Sure, I hit some bad shots, but they usually went in the right direction and I didn't have time to ponder the bad shot, as Tom soon wanted to know all about the next shot I had to play.

By becoming my own virtual caddy, I had to look at the shot I was about to play, as if I was that caddy – in NLP terms I had to be dissociated, in the position of an interested observer. When I actually swung the club, I was back in myself and mentally associated.

How does this help me? Well, the next time you play golf, imagine that you have a "Tom", or whatever name you want to call him or her, in your head, acting as your virtual caddy and asking you to describe the shot you're about to play, in great detail. It's easier to remember, if you get your "Tom" to ask about every shot and every putt. After a few rounds, he'll always be there, helping you.

If you don't believe me, then just try this experiment.

Step 1: Imagine you're on a golf course that you know well and you're facing a particularly difficult shot. Maybe it's one you always find difficult.

Being "Your Own Virtual Caddy"

Step 2: Remember the scene in as much detail and as vividly as possible. What can you hear and where's the sound coming from? Are there any particular smells or aromas? How are you feeling, right now?

Step 3: If you're like I used to be, you're beginning to feel uneasy – perhaps you're starting to panic.

Step 4: I don't know if you've noticed a few other things. Maybe your pulse is starting to race or your breathing has got quicker and shorter as you remember past disasters with this specific shot or others like it. You may even feel a little flushed.

Step 5: And you're likely to hit another bad shot right now, aren't you?

Step 6: Feels bad doesn't it? It's certainly doesn't feel conducive for a smooth relaxed and confident shot.

Now try it another way.

Step 1: Just imagine that you have your own "Tom" advising you and encouraging you. Picture him and imagine the sound of his "voice" and his calm approach to giving you advice, guidance and above all relaxed confidence. Imagine how you'd feel discussing things with your "Tom".

Step 2: Really feel that you're there with your "Tom" and then assess the shot together. Thinking about the distance, the lie, the landing area, the wind and temperature, how you're playing today and any other things that you'd like to take into account.

Step 3: Finally, you're ready to agree on your club choice, your target and the shot you're going to play.

Step 4: Now imagine hitting that shot just as you've planned. First, step back out of yourself and "see" yourself hitting the shot, like watching another you doing it, and watch the ball travelling to the target.

Step 5: If you're happy with that imagined "shot", then step back into your body and imagine executing the same swing. This time, it's you hitting the ball, feeling the smoothness of the swing, hearing the sound of the club striking the ball and then turning your head to see the ball flying perfectly to your target.

Step 6: That feels good, doesn't it? You should be feeling confident and upbeat about being well prepared to physically hit that shot.

Once you get used to having your version of "Tom" as your virtual caddy, you can start to get him to help you in other ways. But forget about him carrying the bag though, he's not real – physically. He's just a very real idea in your mind.

So what else could you get "Tom" to do for you? Well, as a part of your unconscious programming, he's always there when you need him, reminding you to do those things you tend to forget, like your pre-shot routines.

He can also help you to concentrate when you need to in a round of golf and to relax when you don't need to. Like willpower, you can only really keep your concentration going for a few minutes at a time and you take a lot longer than that to play a round of golf. You may also want to break your concentration to enjoy the company of other players or just to relax and appreciate the scenery.

Golf is not a game of certainty. If it was, the phrase "rub of the green" wouldn't exist. Your "Tom" can help you get over that as well and take the sting and anger out of your occasional bad shots.

Using your Foursomes or Fourball Partner as "Your Own Virtual Caddy"

Many, many years ago, I was selected to play with a good friend of mine as my partner in the Hertfordshire County Foursomes team event at the old East Herts. Golf Club, a course I had never played before. Despite my best endeavours, I didn't have the time to play the course before the event, so I had to play it blind. When I got there, there were no yardage charts available and no distance yardage markers on the course, so my foursomes partner, who had played there several times and knew the course well, suggested that he would have to tell me where to hit the ball when it was my turn to hit our ball, as there were many doglegs and blind shots on the course. In other words, he became the embodiment of *"My Own Virtual Caddy"*. It helped that he knew

Being "Your Own Virtual Caddy"

my game well and we played off similar handicaps. Maybe he was a bit better as a golfer than me, even without my help!

On every shot I had to play, my partner would tell me the length and style of shot I needed to play and give me a specific target to aim at – a particular tree, bunker or part of a building. And that was all I had to think about. He never told me about any of the hazards to avoid. As a result, I was the perfect partner, hit the ball where and how he told me and we scored far better than we could have possibly expected.

"Your Own Virtual Caddy" Golf Hypnosis Programme

At the time of writing this book, the 25 minute "Your Own Virtual Caddy" golf hypnosis recording is available to download at no cost as an mp3 file to anyone who subscribes to the free Golf Hypnotist Ezine at *www.golf-hypnotist.com*. The transcription of this recording is included as Appendix 3 to this book.

The good news is that "Your Own Virtual Caddy" already includes post-hypnotic suggestions for focussing your concentration, when you start planning each shot, and for relaxing your focus and concentration, as you release it. So just listening regularly to the recording should help you to unconsciously relax or concentrate appropriately when you need to, without you consciously having to remember.

If you're like most people listening to the "Your Own Virtual Caddy" recording, you will be comfortably in hypnosis by the time you get to these post-hypnotic suggestions and your conscious mind will be unaware of them. As a result, the suggestions will pass straight through to your unconscious mind for consideration. If that's the case, then the recording will work even better, as you won't be consciously looking out for the suggestions to work. If you do consciously remember the suggestions, it doesn't matter. You can just forget about them and simply enjoy your new instinctive approach to golf. And you'll be pleasantly surprised at how much you're relaxing and enjoying your game.

What if I already have a real live caddie, Andrew? Well, it depends on the caddie! If you've already got a high class caddy, like Ronan Flood, Fanny Sunesson or Steve Williams, and you still need help then I probably need to work personally with both of you. If your caddy just carries your bag and hands you your clubs and you're happy with that, then you should listen regularly to the recording, get a new caddie or do both.

I wrote and recorded "Your Own Virtual Caddy" for the vast majority of my readers, professional and amateur alike, who don't yet have the luxury of a super-star caddie.

Technique: Homework for Your Own Virtual Caddy

Using the "Your Own Virtual Caddy" recording or transcription will be a great help to your golf and you can get additional benefit by doing a bit of homework. This task gives you the experience of consciously thinking about and planning every shot, rather than just walking up and hitting it. As a caddy, you don't get to hit the shot yourself and have to hand over that task to someone else – just like trusting your unconscious abilities.

So all you have to do is to caddy for someone else for a few holes or ideally a full round. Alternatively get somebody to caddy for you. If you're not sure what caddying involves, then go to a tournament or watch one on TV. Focus on the interaction between player and caddy.

Once you know roughly what to do then here's a few different approaches, in descending order of effectiveness.

1. Caddy for a golf professional.
2. Caddy for a good amateur golfer.
3. Caddy for a friend – the better they are as a golfer, the better the results and they may benefit as well.
4. Watch top professional golfers like Rory McIlroy, Phil Mickelson and Tiger Woods in tournaments on TV and imagine being their caddy.
5. Imagine a round of golf with you as your own caddy.

When you work at it, you may suddenly surprise and delight yourself by finding your golf improving dramatically with the unconscious help of your own virtual caddy.

Chapter 13

The Secrets of Hypnotic Putting

> *"I've heard people say putting is 50 percent technique and 50 percent mental. I really believe it is 50 percent technique and 90 percent positive thinking, see, but that adds up to 140 percent, which is why nobody is 100 percent sure how to putt."* – Chi Chi Rodriguez

I work, using Golf Hypnosis, NLP and EFT, with different clients on almost every aspect of the game of golf, from putting psychology and the Yips through to concentration and lack of confidence. My clients often go on to seeking my help with their lives in general. With so many common factors, you could be forgiven for assuming that there's a standard "cure" for each problem or opportunity a client may bring. The good hypnotherapist sees each client as the unique person they are, with their own set of unique issues and expectations, and develops a tailored approach for that client.

Nowhere is this more true than with putting, the game within the game of golf. Putting is the great leveller in golf and we all have the opportunity to be a great putters, regardless of age, sex, build, health and level of fitness. Putting also accounts for approximately a third to a half of our total score. The lower your handicap, the larger the proportion of your score will be putts.

Golfers typically take as many as thirteen other clubs with them when playing golf, and yet it's rare to see anyone take more than one putter. In addition, most of those other clubs are pretty similar to everyone else's. My 3-Wood is unlikely to be substantially different from your one in terms of length, loft, size, shape or weight and the same is true for every other club in the bag – apart from the putter. How many times have you played in a fourball and every player had the same style of putter, let alone the same model. Do you often come across mallet-headed drivers, centre-shafted woods, broomstick sand wedges or long-irons with two-thumb grips? Yes, I know those are against the rules!

You're also likely to see much greater diversity in how people stand, grip and swing their putters than you ever see with the rest of the clubs. That's probably why Dave Pelz, one of the leading short game experts, can usefully take 387 pages in his Putting Bible to explain the complexities of the "flat stick". So it should be no surprise that there's no one-size-fits-all approach to putting psychology. Any good work here needs to be interactive and iterative.

Putting Psychology equals Golf Psychology

Everything I've written about golf psychology in this book applies equally well to putting as to any other shot in golf. In addition, regardless of age, strength and level of fitness, everyone who plays golf has the physical attributes necessary to become one of the best putters in the world.

One building block that becomes even more important with putting is visualisation, especially the three-dimensional aspects of the slope, contour and any grain of the green. We can also see every inch of our chosen line to the hole when putting. That means we have the opportunity to visualise the full rolling path of the ball and, very importantly, the direction the ball will be travelling as it enters the hole. Many good putters, when they visualise their shot in their pre-shot routine, see the line the ball travels as it rolls from their putter along their chosen path and falls into the hole. Some see it as an imaginary line, just like the overlay graphics the television commentators use when they show the anticipated line of someone's putt.

Some people see this imaginary line as they take their final look at the hole in their shot routine, just before they move their eyes back to the ball and stroke the putt. I read somewhere that immediately before he hits the putt, Jack Nicklaus sees the ball roll from his putter along his chosen line, fall into the hole, then pop back out and roll back along the same line to the putter. It certainly seemed to work for him.

Expanding your peripheral vision and awareness, detailed in the next chapter, is also especially helpful when reading your putts, as it allows your unconscious mind to take in all the information about the slope and contour of the green at the same time. You can then use your much narrower field of foveal vision to focus on the fine detail of your chosen path to the hole, if you need to.

Remember and enjoy being a good putter

There were some amazing golf and putting psychology lessons on show during Phil Mickelson's stunning win at the 2009 Tour Championship at East Lake. His victory was both breathtaking and more importantly joyous, given the diagnosis of cancer earlier in the year for his wife and his mother. Although they were recovering well, Phil had been looking out of sorts in recent weeks. After his quadruple bogey 8 on the 14th hole in the first round, things didn't look any better for the weekend.

You may recall hearing about Phil's putting woes at the time and his comments about how *"I've hit the ball so well and yet my scores haven't reflected that."* You probably also recall hearing about how "Bones" Mackay, Phil's longstanding caddie, urged him to get help the week before the Tour Championship from Dave Stockton, one of the best putters in golf and twice a major winner. As if those weren't sufficient reasons, Stockton also putts a bit like Phil does when he's at his best.

So what major flaws did Dave Stockton notice in Phil's putting stroke and what major changes did he prescribe? You'd expect them to be fairly severe given Phil's recent comments about the inconsistent putting that had plagued him off and on over the last two years. He's also talked about how his poor putting had detracted from the progress Butch Harman's been making with his swing over the same period.

Well, Phil described the putting change in an interview as a *"minor tweak"* and went on to say *"No, it's very minor. It's very* minor. But [my] hands are back ahead like I used to putt, and the ball is just rolling much better." In another interview, he talked about Dave Stockton's comments just *"reaffirming the way I've putted since I was a kid."*

So what golf psychology lessons can we learn from that? Well first of all, it confirms that if you've hit a particular shot well in the past, then you already unconsciously know how to hit it that well again – without changing your technique. All you need to do is to vividly recall one of those earlier successful shots and allow your unconscious golf mind to get on with the job as you get back into your comfort zone. I'd certainly include this type of visualisation in your pre-shot routine.

All that had probably happened to Phil was that he missed a few putts, lost his confidence and started to fear putting rather than enjoying the challenge. When that happens with any part of our golf game, we stop enjoying ourselves as much as we did and we start consciously analysing things. It doesn't take too long before we start thinking there's something drastically wrong with our swing or putting stroke and we start changing things, even though we seemed to have a perfectly effective method before.

This doesn't just happen over a long period of time. For many of us it can happen in the middle of a round. Have you ever had the experience of playing a series of shots quite well and then hitting a bad shot, maybe a big slice? Did you badly pull or hook the next shot? If you did something like that, you probably consciously thought you needed to make a swing correction, despite already knowing how to hit the ball quite well unconsciously. Well, you did agree that you'd hit a series of shots quite well, didn't you.

Another golf psychology lesson was written on Phil Mickelson's face all day on that Sunday at East Lake, not just when he'd won. He was clearly enjoying himself immensely, even before he started scoring well. After the round, he commented that, *"Today was a lot of fun"* and that's not the way he'd been talking in recent weeks. Isn't it odd how we golfers seem to play so much better when we're enjoying ourselves?

The Secrets of Hypnotic Putting

Reframe yourself as a good putter

I wrote extensively in Chapter 7, *Positive Framing on the Golf Course*, about how to positively reframe the content and context of what life in general and golf in particular throws at you. That clearly has a big beneficial impact on your state of mind. But how do you handle the negative impact of things that have already happened? You can eliminate the immediate negative effect of a less than perfect shot in your post-shot routine, perhaps by using Nick Faldo's "reset button". But what do you do when someone or something later reminds you about that bad shot? How do you manage your state then?

Well, as I've said, successful people take the learnings from a negative experience and then let go of it. They dwell on the things they do well, they replay them in the theatre of their mind over and over, thus creating neural pathways which allow them to recreate their excellence. A story about Jack Nicklaus illustrates this perfectly.

Apparently, Jack was speaking at a fund-raising dinner at Georgia Tech, where his son Michael was studying. During the speech, Jack makes the comment that he has never three putted the last hole of a tournament or missed from inside of three feet. As Jack opens the floor to take questions, a man puts up his hand and says to Nicklaus.

"Jack you say you have never missed from inside of three feet on the last hole of a tournament, but I was watching you last month in the US Seniors PGA and that's exactly what you did." Jack looked at the man with those piercing blue eyes and repeated that he had never missed from inside of three feet on the last hole of a tournament. *"But Mr Nicklaus"*, the man insisted, *"I saw it, I have it on film, I can send it to you if you like"*. *"No need"*, Jack replied, *"I have never missed from inside of three feet on the last hole of a tournament. Are there any more questions?"*

Now, has Jack Nicklaus ever missed from inside of three feet on the last hole of a tournament? Of course he has! Does he remember it? Not a chance. And do you think he cares that he can't remember? Well, yes he does care passionately about the benefit of not remembering his bad shots.

Some people would probably say that Jack is deluded in his thinking and that it is not based on reality. Well, we all create our own reality and wouldn't it be better for our golfing realities to be more like Jack's than almost anyone else's?

Our internal representations are not always concerned with past memories. We can just as easily play constructed ones on the cinema screen of our mind. These can be images of what may or may not occur in the future. Again, this can have a tremendous impact on the state we encounter in the present moment.

It becomes almost second nature for many people to unconsciously play out images of impending disaster for upcoming events, be they golfing or otherwise. The only way that a player can get really anxious before an event is to watch movies in the theatre of his mind which have particularly unsuccessful results. Often, a player will see themselves playing a particular hole badly. They maybe imagine what their "friends" may say when they have finished. They may remember a previous occasion when they felt very nervous and vividly recall that feeling. As they keep doing all of this, without any real conscious awareness, they wonder why many golfers feel a spreading sense of impending doom about the upcoming round, shot or putt.

The best players, in business, life and golf, see impending realisable success. That's good state control!

The Yips

> "The yips are that ghastly time when, with the first movement of the putter, the golfer blacks out, loses sight of the ball and hasn't the remotest idea of what to do with the putter or, occasionally, that he is holding a putter at all." – Tommy Armour

Thankfully, I know that most of my readers aren't suffering with the Yips. So for those lucky ones, I suggest you have a close look at the *Six Steps to Swishing away the Yips* technique below, as

The Secrets of Hypnotic Putting

it works equally well on any other less than desired issue, habit or belief in your golf game or elsewhere in your life.

I'm always surprised at the number of people who first come to me about the problems their experiencing with the Yips – either with their putting, their chipping or both. It must account for around half of all the people who contact me through my www.golf-hypnotist.com website and about half of those specifically want help with their chipping and half with their putting. I have to tell you that the emails I receive from people about their Yips are often pretty traumatic. That makes it all the more satisfying when I help them overcome their problem.

Now this shouldn't surprise me, as some very famous players have talked about their problems with the Yips. A lot more have kept their affliction to themselves and suffer in silence. Some, like Bernhard Langer have successfully overcome the Yips while other greats, such as Sam Snead, Harry Vardon and Ben Hogan took the problem to their graves. Hogan is even said to have campaigned for a change in the rules of golf to reduce the value of putts to half a shot.

Sam Snead won a record 82 events on the PGA Tour in his career, more than either Jack Nicklaus or Tiger Woods, so far. He also won a further 50 tournaments around the world. How many more might he have won if he hadn't had to resort to putting croquet-style between his legs half way through his career? Bearing in mind that he still managed to shoot his age with a 67 in a PGA Tour event 33 years after his problems started.

Despite being a relatively poor putter, Harry Vardon won 6 British Open Championships and is well known for the Vardon Grip and the Harry Vardon Trophy. That's traditionally awarded to the winner of the European Tour Order of Merit and in 2009 to the winner of the Race to Dubai. Despite all this success, Vardon developed the Yips during his career.

Although there still seem to be as many amateurs admitting that they suffer with the Yips as ever, you more rarely hear reports of players on the US PGA and European Tours suffering in the same way. So why is this? Well here are a few thoughts.

1. If they suffer form the Yips early on in their career, they rarely succeed in getting on the Tour.
2. Most top players now use golf psychologists and/or hypnotists, so they find a "cure" that works for them
3. More players use long putters, belly putters and strange grips early in their careers these days and it's become more acceptable.

Now for the good news, I have great success helping people overcome the yips using a variety of golf psychology and NLP techniques and, of course, golf hypnosis. What's interesting is that my clients often have to use several different techniques before they find a combination that works for them. Having said that, I have found that the NLP Swish pattern almost always features in that combination and that's why I've included it below.

The other item of good news is that I haven't worked with anyone who has a physical impediment that actually causes their Yips. It always seems to be a problem in their golfing minds that they can overcome with my help. Now, I'm not saying that there aren't people out there with physiological or neurological reasons for their problems, just that I don't come across them.

Remember that if mercifully you don't have the yips, the next section could still have something in it for you, so read please on.

Technique: Six Steps to Swishing away the Yips

Start by finding a safe, comfortable and quiet place to sit or lie down, where you'll be free from any interruptions for a while. Make sure that your mobile and any other phones in the room are muted or simply turned off. Now, if you're familiar with self-hypnosis, then use your preferred technique to take you into a nice relaxing hypnotic trance with a receptive and imaginative mind. Alternatively, you can achieve the same with either the *Finger Breathing* or the *Betty Erickson* self-hypnosis technique included in Chapter 2, *Hypnosis and Self-Hypnosis for Golf*.

Step 1: Think of a time when you hit a particularly bad chip or putt and imagine you are back there at that time. See through your own eyes what you saw then, as vividly as you dare. Imagine a border around the picture and hold it, in your mind's eye, right in front of you and make the picture bold and intense. Remember how bad it felt at the time. You can close your eyes to do all this, if you prefer. Park this bad shot image in the back of your mind.

Step 2: Now think of a time when you hit a really good shot. If you can't remember one, imagine a future time when you can hit a really good one. This time, see it as if you're watching yourself hitting that good shot. Make the picture bright and bold. Amplify the colours. Hear the good things you're saying to yourself and the supporting comments of your playing partners. Notice how you're acting and imagine how good you must be feeling as you watch yourself play this wonderful shot.

Step 3: Now shrink this good shot image down to a small dark postage stamp size and place it in the bottom corner of the bad shot image.

Step 4: Now, as fast as you possibly can, darken and shrink the bad shot image down, while you brighten and enlarge the good shot image until it completely covers the bad picture. At the same time, hear or make the sound "sar-wish" just as quickly as you swish the picture.

Step 5: Now break state by concentrating hard on something other than golf for 30 seconds or more – your family, your work, the weather, another hobby or anything but golf.

Step 6: Now recall the two pictures and go back and repeat steps 3 to 5 a further four times, remembering to break state between each one.

Finally, imagine you're playing a tricky chip or putt, in a future round, and notice how confident you feel now. If you want to make it even better, then repeat the 6 steps either now or if you ever feel you need a top-up.

There's a big added bonus here too, as you can use this NLP swish technique for any other problem area, habit or belief that you'd like to change in your golf or elsewhere in your life.

Technique: Other ways of Overcoming the Yips

There are many other golf psychology approaches to overcoming the Yips including:

Looking at the Hole – Putt while looking at the hole or your target point, rather than at the ball. The separation of the conscious task of looking for the result and the unconscious task of swinging the putter certainly helps me when I use this technique.

Holing putts in your mind – Relax in a comfortable location, recalling and replaying as many good putts from your past or imagining what they would have been like. You can read more about practicing in your mind in Chapter 21, *Playing and Practicing Golf in your Mind*.

Never "really" miss a putt – When you hole a putt, replay it in your mind, both at the time and later when you review your practice session or round. If you miss a putt, just imagine that you holed it and replay the imagined successful putt in your mind. This is similar to the story above about Jack Nicklaus never missing a key short putt.

Tap away the Yips – Another, possibly even weirder, approach is to use a technique called EFT, the Emotional Freedom Technique. Some people say it's like acupuncture, except you tap the meridian points with your finger rather than using needles! For me it works in a similar way to hypnosis, in that you consciously have to focus on the tapping sequence while you unconsciously think about the problem you want to correct – the Yips. At the time of writing this book, you can download the free *EFT Get Started Pack* from Gary Craig's website at *www.emofree.com/downloadeftmanual.asp*.

Part 3

On the Course and Between Shots

Chapter 14

State Management in Golf

"The person who is able to control his own state will, to a large extent, be able to control his world and the results he achieves within that world" – Tiger Woods

People often say that the way we live our lives reflects the way we practice our hobbies, sports and pastimes. The way we live in our business life is certainly reflected in the way we play golf. The depths of our character, good and bad, are hard to hide during a game of golf. Perhaps that's why so much business seems to be conducted on the golf course. Maybe it allows the opportunity to develop a form of rapport or is just a way of seeing the real person we are doing business with.

But maybe we can break the mould and change the way our brains are wired. Maybe we can change for the better and play better golf. Better golf in a better mental state.

There's certainly one man in golf who's known how to control his mental state. And that's Tiger Woods. In 2008, he won his 3rd US Open and his 14th Major Championship despite having all the excuses in the world. Anybody who saw him play that year will know that he was in great pain from his recent knee surgery. But his control of his mental state saw him through, despite him having to hobble through an extra eighteen holes in the play-off. The damage was sufficient for him to need more surgery.

Most people are operating at the mercy of their constantly changing states. That's, because most people don't know how to control the way they feel. Their state is usually determined by what is happening in the outside world or their perception of it – their personal map of reality. If it is a nice sunny day, they feel good. If the golf ball is "behaving itself", they feel confident. If the person they are playing with is to their liking, they feel happy. The way they feel, their state, is often controlled by external events – events that are beyond their control.

While you may not have control over many of these external events, you do have the opportunity to control your own personal reaction to these events. The ability to get into the right state, at the right time, for the task or experience at hand, is very important for successful golf. It's the fundamental difference between the people who achieve their goals and live fulfilled lives and those who don't.

So how do you get into your desired state? Well, you go in and out of a whole range of states of mind and body all day long. These states can vary from relaxed to frustrated, calm to angry, open to learning to shut about learning, happy to sad, confident to uncertain and many, many more. Think of how many different states you experience in a typical round of golf.

So what can you do about all this? What can you do to influence and control your states and play better golf – or perform any other pursuit better? There are lots of tools, tips and techniques using NLP and Hypnosis. They all boil down to two key issues – managing your internal representations and your physiology.

Every experience and every thought you have and every state you experience is represented internally in terms of your five main senses – sight, sound, feeling, taste and smell. If you smell a particular smell or hear a particular piece of music, you can be transported back in your mind to some past event, in your "mind's eye". You then experience all the feelings and emotion of that event. If you were feeling confident then, you do again now. Many times, that event will then automatically link in your mind to other times when you were confident. You may experience the event in any, all or some combination of your five senses.

You could imagine that memory or thought being played out as if it was on a cinema or television screen, but with all the other senses and emotions thrown in. This is a cinema that never closes;

even when you're asleep it keeps on going – playing out our dreams. When we watch a good movie or TV programme, we sometimes feel like we are in the scene, feeling all the emotions. It can even affect our physiology. Have you ever noticed how your pulse races at the exciting parts of a thriller or sporting event? For most people, the internal movies keep on running and running, playing out the same old stuff over and over again at the unconscious level and producing the same old results, emotions and unresourceful states.

Technique: Seven Steps to Changing your State, Now

To experience this for yourself, just follow these seven steps.

Step 1: Start by finding a safe, comfortable and quiet place to sit or lie down, where you'll be free from any interruptions for a while. Make sure that your mobile and any other phones in the room are muted or simply turned off.

Now, if you're familiar with self-hypnosis, then use your preferred technique to take you into a very light relaxing hypnotic trance with a receptive and imaginative mind. Alternatively, you can achieve the same with either the *Finger Breathing* or *Betty Erickson* self-hypnosis techniques included in Chapter 2, *Hypnosis and Self-Hypnosis for Golf.*

Step 2: Imagine you've just hit a really bad golf shot, maybe one that costs you a couple of shots. Remember what you said to yourself and most importantly what you felt. What state were you in then and how do you feel thinking about it? Now forget about that shot completely. It never happened.

Step 3: Now just steady your breathing, focus on the moment and begin to engage your amazing mind. Imagine you're out on the tee on your favourite hole of your favourite golf course and with your favourite golf club in your hands. Imagine the scene in any way that suits you. See what you would see, perhaps the layout of the course, the sky, the scenery and maybe other people on the course. Hear the sounds that surround you and feel the contours of the ground, the temperature and any breeze on your face and the feel of your shoes on the grass. I don't know if you can smell the grass or other familiar scents and aromas that take you back to this special scene.

Step 4: Imagine there's a ball on the ground in front of you. I don't know if it's your favourite brand, but it's a good one and it's sitting on a tee at just the right height. And as you look down the fairway or to the green, you just imagine the perfect tee shot for this hole.

Step 5: Without realising it, you've gone through any pre-shot routine you use, taken your stance and you see the clubhead hitting the ball perfectly, as you feel the texture of the grip and hear the crisp sound of a really well hit shot.

Step 6: Now you're watching the ball flying majestically through the air and land in just the way you imagined it. It's just perfect isn't it?

Step 7: And as you pick up the tee and hear the compliments of your playing partners, look again at the result of that amazing shot, and your wonderful sense of achievement.

Now that feels different, doesn't it? How do you imagine you'd hit the next shot in this new state, feeling this good?

So, if you could always play that movie before hitting a golf shot, you would get into a more positive, relaxed, resourceful and confident state, wouldn't you. You would be in control. A bit like Tiger is, perhaps. Most times, you've probably played the wrong movie.

Expand your Peripheral Vision and Awareness

Have you ever noticed the apparently intense visual focus displayed in the eyes of top golfers, such as Padraig Harrington, Seve Ballesteros and Tiger Woods, when planning and playing their shots? Well, I've certainly noticed that "wide-eyed" look from them. And that's why I say apparent visual focus, because that betrays the exact opposite of focus in visual terms. They are wide-eyed because they are extending their peripheral vision as much as they can to increase their peripheral awareness. They want to be aware of everything that's going on around them, especially anything that could influence the shot they are planning to hit.

State Management in Golf

This expanded peripheral vision and awareness is taught in martial arts and on advanced driving courses to help people to be aware of as much of what's going on around them as possible. All good hypnotherapists are taught the same skills, as it helps to be really aware of what's going on with the client. It's the same technique that champion boxer Muhammad Ali experienced and he described it as feeling like he was watching his own fights from above each of the four corners of the ring. It was as if he could "see" his opponents back muscles move long before any signs from the front that a punch was on its way. You often hear people talking people who appear to have "eyes in the back of their head". That's just expanded peripheral awareness.

Most of the time, including the time between playing shots and for most people when they are reading a book, we use our eyes to focus on just one thing, like an individual letter or word in this text. When we do that, we use our foveal vision, involving a very small part of our retina, considerably less than 1% of its total area, which provides exceptionally sharp visual detail to the conscious parts of the mind. The remaining 99% of our visual capacity is primarily used for peripheral vision by our unconscious mind. You're using your foveal vision when you read the words in this book, but if an insect buzzes close to your eye while you're reading, it's picked up by your peripheral awareness and you unconsciously and automatically close your eyes, taking avoiding action without conscious thought.

What's particularly interesting for achieving the ideal state of being in the zone or playing unconscious golf, is that your peripheral vision activates your unconscious. That also calms your mind and suppresses internal dialogue. That's just what's needed for that wide-eyed focus we see from these players. Conversely, when our eyes are physically screwed up, when we concentrate on fine detail and we're using our foveal vision, we tend to get stressed. That's not the ideal state for good golf.

Technique: Seven Steps to more Peripheral Awareness

Here's a simple but effective technique to help you learn how to expand your peripheral awareness and be more peripherally focussed when you're planning and hitting your shots. I strongly recommend that you practice this regularly and incorporate an expanded peripheral awareness into your pre-shot, shot and post-shot routines.

Step 1: You can use this technique effectively, sitting or standing, more or less anywhere. However, it may be best for the first few times to find a safe, comfortable and quiet place to sit, where you'll be free from any interruptions for a while. Make sure that your mobile and any other phones in the room are muted or simply turned off.

Step 2: Notice a small point some distance in front of you and very slightly above eye level. It could be something on the wall or window, if you're indoors, or a tree or flag on the golf course. Now fix all your attention and focus on that one single point exclusively for a few moments, making some fine distinctions in what you see.

Step 3: Now relax your eyes and notice the tendency for your vision to expand. You can see the ground, the ceiling or sky and things either side of you, all at the same time and without moving your head or even your eyes. There is no need to focus in on any particular thing. What you're experiencing is your peripheral vision.

Step 4: As you notice your breathing beginning to shift, maybe becoming deeper and calmer, maybe more rhythmic, take this sense of visual awareness and wrap it around you and behind you like a velvety cloak. You may not be able to see what is behind you, but you can get a sense of what that would be like. Get a sense of being able to feel with your vision, of thinking that your vision extends all around you.

Step 5: Now focus on your hearing. Imagine your ears to be like a bat's sonar organ. Imagine your hearing stretching out in wider and wider circles. Become aware of the things that you hear. Maybe it's people talking, the wind in the trees, the hum of the heating, traffic outside and your own breathing.

Step 6: Now move to your feelings. Imagine your feelings to be centred in your belly. Push your feelings out around you and outwards, like a sphere radiating from your belly. Notice a feeling of almost touching the walls or distant objects with this expanded sense, as you're feeling everything in between. Make sure you know just what that feels like; as you imagine that you really are feeling the space that you're in.

Step 7: Finally, become aware of all three senses – seeing, hearing and feeling – radiating from you in interlocking circles and at the same time. Enjoy this expanded awareness for a while; absorb all that you can with your senses; and truly experience a feeling of what it's like to acutely sense that moment you're in. This is truly being alive! When you have absorbed as much of that as you can, then come back out.

You should be feeling really good after that and you probably look a bit spaced when you're actually playing a shot – just like Padraig, Seve and Tiger. Now just imagine feeling like this every time you plan and play a golf shot.

Chapter 15

Physiology and Between Shots

"If you can't enjoy the time between golf shots, then you're going to have a pretty difficult life because most of your life is the time spent in-between."
– Peter Jacobsen

If I was to ask you what you do between shots during a round of golf, you'd probably think I was missing the point. After all, golf psychology and swing coaching should be all about helping you to hit better shots and putts during a round of golf or in practice, shouldn't it? This applies whether you're working with a teaching pro helping you with your golf swing or with a golf psychologist helping to improve your mental approach to golf.

So what do you actually do in the time between assessing and hitting your shots and putts? It really should take a lot less than a minute on average to size up a shot, decide on how to play it, set up to the ball and hit it. I seem to recall from somewhere that the US PGA allows 30-45 seconds per shot for all this and very few people take that long over a short putt. So all that should add up to a maximum of 54 minutes to go round in 72 strokes and 72 minutes to go round in 90 strokes. That means that if you take just 4 hours to play a round, then you're not actually playing for approximately 3 hours in every 18 holes.

Are you head-down, trudging round the course?

What many people do in this spare 3 hours in every round is to get down on themselves mentally. Just watch how many golfers trudge between shots with their heads down and seemingly just staring at the ground a few feet ahead. Many of them are talking to themselves and often what they are saying is not fit for publication. Thankfully, they normally keep the voice inside their heads, but I'm sure you've played the odd round with a playing partner who berates himself loudly between shots. I know I've done that in the, hopefully distant, past and I'm not proud of it.

So what's wrong with keeping your head down between shots? Well just watch how people typically stand when their life is on the up. Yes, they stand and walk erect with their heads held high and their shoulders back. Psychological research also demonstrates that this works the other way too, so if you walk between shots with your head down and your shoulders a bit slumped, you'll automatically feel down.

As Ross Fisher showed us at the 2009 Open Championship at Turnberry, you don't have to drop your head just because you hit a rough patch. A very thick rough patch in his case, but he just kept on with his head raised high and continued positively as he played the remaining holes in par. Maintaining this upright confident posture will have quite an impact on your fellow competitors as well. Have you noticed how the confident postures of Tiger Woods, Jack Nicklaus or Seve Ballesteros in his prime, seemed to intimidate their opponents. It's the same in other sports, like cricket. Have you ever seen a successful Australian cricket team walking round without a confident swagger? Shane Warne immediately comes to mind with his mixture of overt, undisguised boldness and covert, disguised baldness.

At the other extreme, have you ever noticed how depressed many people in nursing homes seem to be and how many of them walk around in a bent-over posture? Well I met a husband and wife recently, both doctors, who are incorporating NLP concepts into body work. They've found that they can improve the posture and, more importantly, increase the level of happiness and optimism of patients in nursing homes. They often achieve this by simply replacing the lounge chairs with ones that encourage a more upright sitting posture. They also hang televisions from the ceilings rather than sitting them near the floor, so that people have to look

Physiology and Between Shots

up. Those simple changes lead to wholesale improvements in people's posture, health and happiness.

Next time you play golf; walk between shots with your back straight and your head held high. You could even add to that by using one of the self-hypnosis techniques from Chapter 2, *Hypnosis and Self-Hypnosis for Golf*, or an NLP resource anchor from Chapter 3, *NLP Anchoring for Better Golf*. One of these will help you remember not to forget to do it when you play. However you're actually feeling when you start and regardless of any bad shots you hit, I suspect you'll be amazed at how much better and more positive you'll feel as the game progresses. It may well have an impact on your enjoyment of this wonderful game of golf and, who knows, you may even score better.

One of the best ways to maintain this positive yet relaxed focus while you're walking between shots or maybe waiting for the hole in front to clear, is to simply broaden your peripheral awareness and be at one with nature. After all, most golf courses are visually stimulating and, given fair weather, good places to be. As Walter Hagen once said, *"Don't hurry. Don't worry. You're only here for a short visit. So don't forget to stop and smell the flowers along the way."*

Shouldn't I be concentrating between shots as well?

Have you noticed how some of the world's best golfers play better, more competitively and even more consistently when they are part of a team, than when they are playing for themselves? I'm thinking here about players like Paul McGinley, Darren Clarke, Jose Maria Olazabal and many others. A few others don't seem to fit so comfortably into the team game. This applies to the singles matches as well as the specialist formats like fourball and foursome matches that are played by the professionals in the Ryder Cup, Presidents Cup and the Vivendi/Seve Trophy.

Looking back to my own more humble experience as a 2-handicap amateur in my 20's and 30's, I know that I was more consistent and determined when I was playing for a team, even if it was just my fourball or foursomes partner on a Sunday morning. It became even more relevant when I was playing for my club and county. Not only did I focus harder on my own shots, I also got involved in my partner's game as well and that seemed to both relax me and help me concentrate at a higher level than I achieved when I was just playing for my own score.

So why do we generally play better and certainly harder for our teammates than we do for ourselves? Well for a long time I thought it was all about the camaraderie and the positive desire to support the collective interest of the team. I even considered that it could be the greater pressure of being accountable to other people. After all, I was only letting myself down if I played badly on my own.

In those days, I felt that my priority was to play well at the highest level I could achieve. That meant entering open amateur tournaments and playing for my club and county. As a result, I didn't think that much about the more informal team games I played in, like company golf days. However, I always seemed to really enjoy playing in them, nearly always played well and often brought home the winning team.

Since I got into golf psychology in the last decade, I've started analysing and modelling all the positive aspects of my performance. That has included all the games I played, especially the one's I enjoyed – those company golf days at courses like Moor Park, Wentworth, Denham and Woburn. What I discovered was that I concentrated less on my own game in those company golf days, playing for my partners, and relaxed far more than I did when I was playing for myself.

I came to realise that, when I played in a company golf day, I took responsibility as either the company host or the low-handicap man in the three or fourball team. I also had a business responsibility to talk to my playing partners and make sure they had a good day. As a consequence, I concentrated hard on my own shots and then immediately switched my focus to the more relaxing task of helping my higher-handicap partners. Although this would appear to be a distraction, I always seemed to be able to focus back on my own shots. After all, I wanted to play well for the team and I also wanted them to enjoy playing well themselves.

Physiology and Between Shots

Now imagine my surprise when I read recently about the experience of European Tour player Philip Archer. He had a reputation for winning the pro-am events on the Wednesdays before the main tournaments and he often won them with a course record. He'd then score badly on Thursday and Friday and miss the cut. His problem was finally diagnosed as over-concentration. When he played in the pro-ams, he concentrated briefly on his own shot and then hurried over and focussed his attention on the amateurs. After all, they were paying a lot to be there, so he felt he had a responsibility to help them. As a result he only focussed on his own game when he was planning his shots and hitting his own ball.

When Phil played in the main tournament, he felt that, as a professional golfer, he had to concentrate hard for the whole time he was on the course. The problem was he couldn't keep that intense focus for the 5 hours or more it takes to complete a round on tour. As a result, he didn't play to his full potential and was a nervous wreck by the time he completed his tournament round.

The good news for Phil is that a good golf psychologist pointed this out to him and helped him find a way to relax between shots in the main tournament. Once he did that, he unleashed and fulfilled his potential as a professional golfer by winning on the European Tour.

The good news for the rest of us is that we can use that spare 3 hours or so of each round for relaxation and enjoyment. You can enjoy the scenery, look at the trees or the sky, chat with other people on the course, watch other players or just simply chill out and maybe use some self-hypnosis. Even if you're helping your partner in a foursome, a fourball or maybe a scramble, you're not actually hitting the ball for them, so there shouldn't be any pressure on you, now should there.

What do you say to yourself between shots?

Do you talk to yourself when you're playing golf? Well, if you don't, you may have a serious problem. It's called brain death! Self-talk, otherwise known as internal dialogue or intrapersonal communication, is one of the main functions of our conscious mind. It allows us to make sense of our conflicting thoughts and to express our ideas and feelings to ourselves. Most of the time we talk to ourselves internally and sometimes, particularly after a bad shot, we share our self-talk with everyone in earshot. That can be a large distance with some of the golfer's I've played with!

Many golfers regularly talk to themselves in a negative or even abusive manner while walking down the fairway. With some, it doesn't even seem to matter whether it's a good shot or a bad one! If you use negative self-talk, it's almost certainly spoiling both your enjoyment of the game and your score. The abusive self-talk is often far more offensive than you would normally use in public. Just imagine how you would feel if your fourball partner, foursome partner or your caddy said the same things to you after you hit a bad shot. You'd be horrified and you'd probably make a mental note never to play with them again.

I was surprised to hear Geoff Ogilvy saying that he used to experience negative self talk earlier in his career. In an interview after his victory in the 2009 World Golf Championship Match Play event, he said that in the past, he found it almost impossible to suppress any negative feelings he was experiencing. You wouldn't think that, watching his cool demeanour when playing that week. I found a much older interview where he was talking about how half the Tour talks to themselves badly when they are not playing well. He added that they do it every day and it's very unconstructive. When asked what he meant, he said *"Yeah, just call yourself useless and what are you doing out here and all sorts of stuff. And I was hopeless. And I'm still not the best out here, but I'm getting a lot better."* Clearly Geoff has come a long way since then and I'm sure that golf psychology has had a lot to do with it.

With hypnosis and NLP we can do a lot to channel and manage that negative self-talk. One simple and very effective technique from NLP is just to give that negative voice in our head a silly or a sexy accent. For example, it would be hard to take the negative self-talk if it came from Donald Duck or a seductive Marilyn Munro. You make up the voice in your head, so it's yours to do whatever you want with.

Positive Self-Talk is what you want

Positive self-talk is what you want to be using and it really comes into its own when we are internally analysing and evaluating complex choices in our lives. A good example is when you're starting your pre-shot routine and deciding on the type of shot you're going to play. Have you ever had one voice in your head proposing an ambitious shot with a driver and another one encouraging you to make a more conservative shot with an iron? Don't worry about it. It's perfectly normal and unlikely to be a symptom of schizophrenia!

Now, I've often written about the concept that whatever we consciously think about our unconscious mind does it's best to deliver. And self-talk is the most powerful and influential mechanism for conscious thought. So if you talk to yourself about the bunker you're trying to avoid, rather than the green you should be aiming to hit, your unconscious is likely to put you in the bunker! So it's important to think and talk to yourself positively about your target and your desired shot – the one you visualised earlier, perhaps.

What you say to yourself after you hit your shot is just as important as what you say when you're hitting the shot. Internal communication has a really significant impact on your mood, attitude and effectiveness. It also impacts on those around you. Berating yourself angrily is only going to make you feel bad and anchor that bad feeling to the shot. That means that you're likely to relive that same feeling the next time you have a similar shot to play and you consequently hit an equally bad shot. It's important to learn from a bad shot, as long as you do it positively and then release it to the past where it can't hurt you. I really love Nick Faldo's TV metaphor about Tiger Woods "Hitting the Reset Button" after a bad shot during the Tour Championship.

Positive self-talk is even better for you than negative self talk is bad for you. So talk positively to yourself about the shot you're about to play. One of the best ways to do this is to talk to yourself about the shot you want to play, visualise your target and the shot vividly and think about your visualised shot as you hit the ball. It's difficult to allow negative self-talk to enter your head when you're focussing totally on something positive.

The same applies to your post-shot routine, especially after you've hit a good shot. Relish your good shots, feel really good about them, review them vividly in your mind and tell yourself how good they are. That way, you anchor that good feeling to the shot and you'll feel really good the next time you have a similar one to play.

Now, I think you'll agree that positive self-talk is what you're looking for and the only person you can rely on to say those positive things is you.

Chapter 16

Fear of Golfing Failure and Success

"You're born with only two fears: the fear of falling and the fear of loud noise. All the rest is learned. And it's a lot of work!" – Richard Bandler, creator of NLP

Fear on the golf course can come in many shapes and sizes and it can result in a multitude of problems. These can range from lack of enjoyment, through poor scoring and frustration to outright anger. Most golfers will have experienced fear on the golf course at some time, either when playing themselves or when watching a playing partner play.

As an amateur golfer, my golf is very important to me. However, my livelihood does not depend directly on my ability to score well. However, I can recall many times, especially in my younger days, when I was uncomfortable, nervous, scared and downright terrified on the golf course.

I'm talking here about the sort of feelings I experienced when I arrived on the first tee and found I was playing with some or other golfing celebrity. I'll never forget Bill Shankland, my then golf coach, asking me to stand in for him in a game in late-June of 1970. Bill explained that he was injured and could I take his place in a friendly fourball the following day. He went on to explain that there'd be no pressure as I was playing at my home club and partnering the club pro, Colin Christison, a man I'd played with many times before. Bill also mentioned that one of our opponents would be Ian Connelly from Welwyn Garden City, later to become Nick Faldo's first coach and someone I'd had a few lessons from. I was a bit nervous playing with these two pros that I'd watched playing in the Agfa tournament at Stoke Poges, but I knew them both and felt I could handle it.

The next day, I got to the club and as I joined my playing partner Colin walking to the first tee, I noticed that there was quite a crowd of my fellow club members behind the tee. I nearly collapsed when I walked through the crowd and Colin introduced me to our other opponent. It was Tony Jacklin, back in the UK to prepare to defend his British Open title after winning the US Open a few weeks earlier. I was terrified and it took a lot of quiet calming words from Colin to get me through the first nine holes. I started to enjoy the experience as I loosened up on the second nine.

Like most people back in the early 70s, I had no knowledge of golf psychology and the best advice available was to pull yourself together and get on with it. That was difficult and the effect didn't last!

I'm sure that I would still be very nervous if I found myself unexpectedly playing with a US or British Open Champion. The difference, now that I have the means to relax myself using a variety of golf psychology techniques and really get the most from the experience, is that I'd probably play my best golf.

So what techniques would I use? Well the quickest technique would be to use my finger-thumb NLP Resource Anchor. That would both relax me and get me into a confident and resourceful state. If I was still nervous, I could use self-hypnosis or some simple deep breathing exercises.

First Tee Nerves

> *"It's just another game of golf, go out there and approach it the right way. Another game of golf in contention, which is what it's all about, getting up in the morning tomorrow there will be butterflies, and that's why I play this game, it's that sort of nervous tension that you always want."* – Padraig Harrington

Have you ever found yourself standing on the first tee feeling so nervous that you can hardly stand up, let alone hit a drive down the

Fear of Golfing Failure and Success

middle of the fairway? I know I have many times and never so markedly as when I stood on the first tee in the Golf Illustrated Junior Vase, a prestigious junior tournament back in the early 1970's and held that year at Hexham in Northumberland. It was an invitation event for promising young players. I know. I still can't work out how I got an invite!

Getting back to the story, or at least the background to the story, I drove the 300 miles up to Hexham the day before the competition with a friend who was also competing and we were paired with a third player for a practice round. Despite both being quite tired, we played quite well and when we got to a particular par 3 hole, my friend hit his tee shot to about 6 feet, before turning to me and challenging me to "get inside that". I swung my 7 iron smoothly and watched the shot land inside my partner's ball and roll slowly into the hole for an ace! I was elated, but when we got back to the clubhouse we had to rush off to arrange our accommodation. Apart from anything else, I didn't have enough money to go into the clubhouse and buy everyone a drink, as was customary. So we sloped off without telling anyone.

The next morning there was quite a crowd around the first tee and when it was my time to tee off I felt a little nervous, but I'd played well in the practice round, so I felt optimistic. My rationalised calmness was shattered when the starter came on to the loudspeaker, announced my name and then told the assembled crowd about how they should be expecting great things from me after my hole in one the previous day! I was suddenly frozen to the ground and couldn't move a muscle. I had to be coaxed by my playing partners to take my turn to drive off. My hands were shaking so much, I could hardly balance the ball on the tee and I only just managed to scuff the ball barely 100 yards down the fairway before rushing off the tee. You guessed it, our playing partner in the practice round had told everyone in the club and the tournament sponsors had paid for a round of drinks in my absence! Thankfully, I can't remember my score that morning, but I seem to remember I played better off the first tee in the afternoon round, after the crowd had more or less drifted away.

Now hopefully, you haven't had such an overwhelming first-tee experience, but I'm sure that many of you will have experienced something ranging from nervousness to sheer terror on the golf course. Maybe you were playing with someone you were trying to impress, like your boss or an important client. Now I think about it, I can think of quite a few other situations in my own experience such as

- stepping onto the first tee at my first open amateur competition, the Raymond Oppenheimer Bowl at Temple Golf Club, and suddenly realising that the starter was the Chairman of the multi-national corporation I worked for – and he recognised me
- being introduced to my playing partner in the Hertfordshire Stag at Moor Park in the 70's – it turned out to be Nick Faldo and it was just a month before he turned pro
- arriving on the first tee at Royal Troon as the guest of a local member and having the Club Captain of this regular British Open venue and his 15 friends insist that we go off in front of them.

I'm sure you're getting the picture by now. So what can we do to calm the nerves and play our best golf in these situations? Well, you won't be surprised that hypnosis has something to do with it. All the panic is driven by our conscious mind in general and that voice in the back of the head saying, "Don't Panic" or *"Danger, danger, danger"*, to quote Rocco Mediate talking about the threat of Tiger Woods at Bay Hill earlier in 2009. So, if we can bypass the conscious mind in a hypnotic way, we can free our unconscious golf mind to get on with what it does best – putting our best swing on the ball.

Now, here are five of the many ways to achieve this, including several I have already detailed in this book.

1. If you're anticipating these problems, you can use the *Seven Steps to Changing your State, Now* technique in Chapter 14, *State Management in Golf.*
2. You can set up and use a powerful resource anchor with the *Five Steps to Anchoring your Resources for Better Golf* from Chapter 3, *NLP Anchoring for Better Golf.*

3. If you know in advance that you may be playing in front of a gallery, then you can plan for it using the *Six Steps to Mirroring your Own Gallery* in Chapter 4, *Enjoying your Golf*.
4. Take a technique from Aikido to "balance" yourself mentally and physically using the *Focus on your Hara to Stabilise your Swing* technique from Chapter 10, *Shot Routines: Hitting the Ball*.
5. Alternatively, you could use this next technique.

Technique: Five Steps to Focussing your Heart Back into your Chest

So, you're standing on the first tee or perhaps out on the course; waiting for your turn to play the shot, while you're very, very nervous; and you're not sure if you can stand up; let alone hit a golf shot. Well here's the good news, all that nervousness and uncertainty is in your conscious mind and your unconscious already knows how to swing the club, doesn't it.

If you're familiar with a quick technique for taking yourself into self-hypnosis, use it now. If not, it really doesn't matter, as this technique will do it for you.

Step 1: Quietly take a few deep breaths noticing how the air you're breathing in is cooling your body and calming your mind and the air you're breathing out is expelling all the tension from your body.

Step 2: If your heart seems to be racing or you feel as if your heart is in your mouth, then just imagine that with each breath in; your heart slowly moves farther back to its proper place in your chest and your heartbeat returns toward its normal regular and comfortable rate.

Step 3: Focus all your attention on the heart area of your chest as you continue to breathe deeper and slower. Feel as if you're channelling all your mental energy back into your heart. Imagine that you're breathing in directly through your chest and notice how each breath is flowing over your heart, cooling it and slowing it down to a strong steady rhythm. And notice a deep sense of relaxation and preparedness spreading through your mind and body.

Step 4: As you continue breathing in around your heart, imagine yourself playing a really good shot, one that you've played before on this hole or a similar one. Remembering in your imagination how good that shot feels now, seeing the ball travelling along your intended path to the hole, hearing the sweet sound of the ball leaving the clubhead and maybe hearing the congratulatory comments of those around you, as you imagine the ball finishing in the ideal position that you choose now.

Step 5: Now go through your regular pre-shot routine and, without hesitation, step forward to the ball, take your usual stance and find yourself unconsciously hitting the ball, just as you're imagining you're now, aren't you.

Fear of Winning

> *"Golf is deceptively simple and endlessly complicated; it satisfies the soul and frustrates the intellect. It is at the same time rewarding and maddening – and it is without a doubt the greatest game mankind has ever invented."* – Greg Norman

Greg Norman showed us at the 2008 British Open that his golf mind is still one of the best in golfing history and his achievements outside his golfing game are also a valuable indicator of just how switched on his mind is. However, that's not always been true for him over the last few holes of major championships.

I really enjoyed the 2009 British Seniors Open Championship at Sunningdale. The Old and New courses are among my all time favourites and they are only 10 miles from my home. I was so delighted to be watching so many of my golfing heroes out there playing just as well as I remembered them doing back in their heydays. People in their 50s and 60s playing that standard of golf is an inspiration to people like me of a similar age, and, like the week before at the Open Championship, it reminded me that I really can't use my age as an excuse for playing less golf.

I found it difficult to choose who to follow and who I really wanted to win. It came down to a choice between Greg Norman and Tom Watson. They are both players I admire and both have

Fear of Golfing Failure and Success

played remarkable golf in major championships in 2008 and 2009. I felt sorry that Tom again missed out after coming so close at the Open. However the person I really wanted to win was Greg Norman. Although Greg has won the Open twice before, I hadn't fully appreciated how many times he had slipped up in the last round of majors. I remember of course his pushed long iron on the final hole of the Masters in 1986 when a par would have got him into the playoff and his turning a six shot lead in the last round there ten year's later into a 5 shot defeat by Nick Faldo.

When I checked the records, it turned out that Greg had just those two Open victories out of 23 majors where he finished in the top 6. In addition he came second in 8 of those majors and third in 4 more. So he clearly has a problem finishing off his major championships.

So what happened at Sunningdale, well Greg was striking the ball awesomely well and his shots were going long and straight. Despite dropping a few shots here and there, that you'd expect from a man who plays so little competitive golf, his short game was just amazing. He was probably playing as well as he did in all those top-six finishes in majors. But when he got to the 16th on that Sunday, needing just one more birdie to tie the lead or two to win outright, he pushed his drive way right just like he had hit that long-iron back at the Masters in 1986. Although he made a miraculous recovery from deep in the trees and hit his third fairly close to the pin, he was out of it and three putted. He was still hitting the ball well on 17 and 18, but he was a defeated man.

As far as I can recall, Greg has never mentioned working with a golf psychologist and sadly it shows at times like these. If he had Tiger's training and could use golf psychology and self hypnosis at these critical times, just imagine how many majors he would have won by now. It's such a shame that Greg doesn't seem to think the same way as Jack Nicklaus obviously did in his heyday, given his quote that I used at the beginning of Chapter 5, *Winning Golf.*

> *"Here you are, starting to get afraid of winning the Open. You're leading by 3 strokes with 8 holes to go. You've obviously played well or you wouldn't be in this*

position. You're still playing well. You're doing something you enjoy, so enjoy it." – Jack Nicklaus

For many people, nervousness is the buzz of competition, whether they are competing against other people, themselves or the golf course they happen to be playing. Personally, I feel that if I'm not nervously shaking when I get near the end of a seriously good scoring round or close game in match play, then I might as well give up golf and go and do something else that excites and inspires me. Jack Nicklaus knew that if you didn't feel nervous toward the end of a tournament you're trying to win, then there's something wrong with you. He thrived on that feeling. It's said that he stopped winning golf tournaments when he no longer got so nervous in competition. And you don't have to be winning the tournament to get that feeling, just enjoying the cut and thrust of competition. If you watched the duel between Tiger Woods and Phil Mickelson during the last round of the 2009 Masters, you'll know just what I mean.

Chapter 17

Anger Management in Golf

"I get upset over a bad shot just like anyone else. But it's silly to let the game get to you. When I miss a shot I just think what a beautiful day it is. And what pure fresh air I'm breathing. Then I take a deep breath. I have to do that. That's what gives me the strength to break the club." – Bob Hope

People bring anger with them to the golf course for a wide variety of reasons that go beyond the frustrations and difficulties of this sometimes challenging game. Although coming to the course angry doesn't help your game, I'm only concerned in this chapter with the anger people generate as a result of their golf.

Apart from any anger you may bring with you to the course, the main causes of anger in golf are from players' reactions to the bad and unlucky golf shots they hit, the anticipation of those shots, the things their opponent does and any outside interference. Although these are all different, if you allow any one of them to make you angry and fail to control it, then you inevitably allow it to harm your golf. It is very important here to understand and accept that, whatever the degree and nature of the provocation, the primary victim of your anger will be you. And only you can decide if you're going to make yourself angry over it.

Anger management is often the initial reason for clients approaching me for help with golf hypnosis. I'm pleased to report that it's often one of the most straightforward and quickest problems for you to overcome. I suppose I shouldn't be surprised, given that NLP and hypnosis are primarily about giving people choices and what the angry golfer lacks is choice. It's acceptable to be annoyed and frustrated when you hit a bad shot, but it's disastrous if you're still annoyed, frustrated or worse when you hit your next shot. That's why it's so important to have an automatic and unconscious Post-Shot Routine that includes learning from your bad shots and then releasing them to the past where they can no longer hurt you. You can read more about releasing your bad shots in Chapter 11, *Post-Shot Routines*.

Technique: Manage your Anger with the Dickens Pattern

The negative consequences of losing your temper nearly always impact the future, particularly when a bad shot you've already hit "causes" you to lose your temper with the resulting anger leading to more bad shots, higher scores and abandoned rounds.

This technique is named after Charles Dickens, the author of A Christmas Carol. It loosely mimics Scrooge's fictional experiences under the guidance of the Ghost of Christmas Future. You will begin to realise why this exercise is called the Dickens Pattern, as you notice that the idea of this exercise is to use self-hypnosis to explore two very real, but imagined, possibilities for your future approach to anger management.

Before you start, recall and consider how you currently react to bad shots and to any other things that cause you to lose your temper on the golf course. Think about the consequential impact your reaction will have on the next shot, the next round or the next year of golf.

Now spend a few moments thinking about how you really would like to change your frustration over hitting a bad or unlucky shot. Maybe you want to think about releasing your bad shots after learning from them, as part of your post-shot routine. It may help to think of Nick Faldo's "reset button" from Chapter 11, *Post-Shot Routines*.

Now thinking about how you would like things to be, follow these simple steps.

Step 1: Start by finding a safe, comfortable and quiet place to sit or lie down, where you'll be free from any interruptions for a while.

Make sure that your mobile and any other phones in the room are muted or simply turned off. Now, if you're familiar with self-hypnosis, use your preferred technique to take you into a nice relaxing hypnotic trance, with a receptive and imaginative mind. Alternatively, you can achieve the same with either the *Finger Breathing* or the *Betty Erickson* self-hypnosis techniques included in Chapter 2, *Hypnosis and Self-Hypnosis for Golf*.

Step 2: Imagine walking down the path of your future life, noticing what you're seeing, hearing, feeling and maybe tasting and smelling as you walk forward. It doesn't have to be cinema perfect. It can be no more detailed than describing the walk to the first tee at your regular golf course, maybe feeling your spikes on the path, hearing the chatter of the other golfers and smelling the fresh-cut grass.

So, as you imagine walking along the path of your future life, notice that every step forwards is a minute, an hour or a day into your future. If you look back, you will notice that your past is there; everything you have ever done or experienced is behind you. Become aware of the temperature, the sights, and the sounds as you enjoy walking along this path. Make it sensory rich as you engage in the idea of really being there.

Step 3: Imagine that a few more steps ahead there is a place where the path splits, one fork goes off to the left and the other off to the right. Pause here for a few moments and have a think. Here, there are two different pathways, two possibilities, two ways that you could choose to go on into two different futures.

If you were to choose the path to the left, you'd continue losing your temper much the same as you've done before. You carry on getting angry after a bad shot, hitting more bad shots and scoring below your capability, in much the same way as you have been doing.

If you were to choose the path to the right, the right path, there are new possibilities, achievements, freedom of mind, positive and progressive results and above all, better and more enjoyable golf. Think about that as you stand here at this place where the path splits. You want to make a decision and commit to one of these paths. Now, before you make that decision, you're going to experience what each path holds for your future.

Step 4: Now, step out onto the path to your left, where you make no changes. Briefly imagine that you're going to play golf angrily, poorly and inconsistently, as you discover your unfulfilled golfing achievements. You experience continuing doing what you have in the past. What will your golf be like in 10 years time?

Step out, as every step you take you get older, days pass, weeks pass. Notice how your body is, how your mind is, how you feel about staying on this path. Walk out into your future to the 10 year point and experience how it feels to carry on doing the same things.

This path is just like today, with one difference: you have ten fewer years remaining in your golfing life. I want you to think about how you will feel in 10 years if you continue doing the exact same things you have done to date. What will your regular golf be like?

Really experience that. See what you see, hear what you hear and feel the feelings. Notice the disappointment, the anger, the frustration and the failure. How does that feel? How do you affect those around you? How do they feel? Absorb every aspect of this path that you can choose to take today. Notice everything that you need to know about what it will be like if you carry on with the same behaviour, putting off change.

When you're ready, drift back to where the path splits and pause for a moment.

Step 5: Now take a step out onto the path to the right. This is the path where you create powerful, progressive change. Notice the sense of freedom in your thoughts, the sense of accomplishment as you walk out 10 years into your future along this right path.

Imagine you're ten years into the future, but this time it's different. Why? Because starting today you actually begin making changes in your golf. Specific intentional changes are not easy. They are intentional because these changes are changes that you're choosing and they are the changes that will cause you to play the golf you want to live, experience and dream about. These changes often mean leaving the current perception of security in order to discover your personal golfing freedom. These are the changes that will bring happiness, enjoyment and satisfaction into your golf. Just go there now. 10 years in the future and having made a decade of progressive changes. Imagine playing the golf you want to play.

How does that feel inside? Do you feel that you have really played golf? See the people of your life. How they feel about you and how they react to you? This is the path of a different choice, a different decision. You have the freedom to be how you want to be.

Absorb all you need from this moment in your future and the positive things that you can learn consciously and unconsciously. Now drift and float back to the place where the path splits.

Step 6: Now that you know and have experienced the two contrasting futures. And you know what your future holds as a result of what you do this very day, so you can make a decision. You can compare and contrast those two futures that can be yours, based on a decision that you make now about how you're going to play your golf.

Imagine reaching deep inside yourself for all the strength and wisdom that you need to make this decision today. As you do so, imagine that when you choose to make that decision, that deep inside your mind you're switching off the alternative path. You're switching off the opportunity to drift back to that place.

Then step out and take your future path. Absorb yourself in the sensations, the feelings, the sights, the sounds and experiences of enjoyable and successful golf. Stay there for a few moments, enjoying your new future, before floating back to the present time. Notice that certain wonderful sense of positive expectation.

Step 7: Open your eyes, begin to plan your future and take action to achieve that outcome. Your unconscious mind now knows what it is working toward. Plan the exact sequence of events that will take you to where you want to be. Have a think consciously about what you can do now and write it down. Notice how you feel excited and optimistic when you do this.

What about bad luck and "Rub of the Green?"

The Augusta National course was very wet ahead of the 2009 Masters and I saw many players mishitting shots, almost certainly as a result of "mud balls", and it was interesting to see the many different reactions from the players. I didn't notice any anger from Kenny Perry when his "mud ball" on the second playoff hole veered off to the left. He was clearly disappointed, but just got on with the job of playing the ball as it lies, without complaint. I suspect he would have said that it was the same for everyone. Maybe that attitude got him into the playoff, even if his mental game seemed to desert him over those last few holes.

Sergio Garcia was at the other end of the spectrum in terms of his reaction and I've never seen him look so unhappy with himself and the course. It was no surprise to hear his negative comments about the course after his final round. One quote really stuck in my mind, *"I don't think it's fair,"* he said. *"It's too tricky. Even when it's dry you still get mud balls in the middle of the fairway. It's too much of a guessing game. They can do whatever they want. It's not my problem. I just come here and play and then go home."* I should stress here that Sergio wasn't the only one complaining and I was delighted to read of his later apologies in the press, as I think he still has the potential to be the true successor to his mentor, the great Seve Ballesteros.

Golfers who complain bitterly about bad luck rarely seem to enjoy their golf that much or perform to their best. I know that before I got into golf psychology I used to suffer in that way. Making the right choices when you experience bad luck is one of the secrets of hypnotic golf. You can find more about handling bad luck on the golf course in Chapter 4, *Enjoying your Golf*, Chapter 5, *Winning Golf*, and Chapter 7 *Positive Framing on the Golf Course*.

Do you anticipate bad fortune?

I can almost understand a player who's struggling with his form coming into a tournament expecting to play badly and possibly feeling angry about the fact that he's not giving of his best. However, I'm really unhappy about a player coming into a

Anger Management in Golf

competition playing well and expecting to be beaten, whatever the reason.

I heard two such negative comments in the run up to the 2009 Bay Hill Classic that Tiger Woods eventually won despite not playing at his absolute best. The first comment came from Sean O'Hair, the man who outplayed Tiger in all the physical and technical aspects of the game that week. Just look at his earlier interview when he said *"It's not like it's The Tiger Show and I'm just out there to watch him. We're trying to win golf tournaments, and he just happens to be that good. But just because he's good doesn't mean we're out there watching him."*

Does that sound like a man who confidently believes he's going to win or even thinks he can win? My hypnotherapy mentor says that anyone "trying" to do something has already accepted the possibility of failure. That surely doesn't lead to self-belief, now does it? You may think that some doubt is reasonable given Tiger's undoubted abilities, but you have to go out believing you're going to win. Otherwise, you'll capitulate just like Sean O'Hair did or, as some players do, get angry. Sean's not alone in this capitulation. You only have to look at the history books. It seems like every time Tiger wins from behind on the last day, the people playing technically as well as or better than him capitulate mentally.

The other negative comment came from Rocco Mediate, who should know better after battling toe to toe with Tiger for 90 holes at the 2008 US Open. Talking about Tiger's performance at Doral, a few weeks before Bay Hill, Rocco's quoted as saying, *"Danger, danger, danger. If he's making one bogey in four rounds, he's obviously hitting it better. We know his short game is the best, but we know he didn't really make a lot of putts. When he does that, that will be the Tiger we know, and that will be the end of the game."* How defeatist is that!

Now I'm not blaming Tiger for this or even the media that hype him up so much, although that must weigh down on his opponents. The real failure has to lie with his opponent's mental preparation. Nearly all of them have highly qualified mind coaches, yet they can't be making the best of the advice they get from them on the course. And then if those mind coaches were worth their salt, their clients would be running on autopilot like Tiger and they are clearly not. It makes you wonder if Tiger's the only one using self hypnosis to reinforce the mental coaching he gets from Jay Brunza.

Chapter 18

Protection from Covert Hypnosis

"I look into their eyes, shake their hand, pat their back, and wish them luck, but I am thinking, 'I am going to bury you.'" – Seve Ballesteros

When I do hypnosis work with clients, whether it's face-to-face or in a recorded golf-hypnosis program, I nearly always include something like "... and you're protected from random thought, random image and random sound from having hypnotic authority for you..." I include these words to reinforce the idea that you don't want any outside agencies, intended or otherwise, to have any impact on the work that we're doing. As an example, if you opened your eyes while still in a trance and saw something unpleasant out of the window or overheard a piece of music with particularly negative words, then you don't want to be influenced by them.

As I mentioned in the Chapter 2, *Hypnosis and Self-Hypnosis for Golf*, you experience many naturally occurring forms of trance, especially when you are very focussed on things, like nervously waiting for your name to be called on the first tee in a competition. At these times you are also vulnerable to external influences, whether they are intended or random. This is especially true when you are facing a crucial or particularly difficult shot. These are times when you need to be protected in just the same way as you are when you're in hypnosis and listening to my words.

Thankfully, you can address these external influences through the use of many of the techniques in this book, most especially through the use of state management, your shot routines and self-hypnosis.

Intentional Distractions and Suggestions

I just seem to keep coming across articles that propose hypnosis as a destructive secret weapon for golf and I disagree most strongly with that approach. However, I do fully agree with the idea of golf hypnosis as a personal secret weapon for better golf and I support many of the author's opening arguments. If he'd put his name in the article, I'd even go so far as thanking him here.

I agree with him when he says that, *"Using hypnosis for golf can be your secret weapon on the course. Hypnosis directs your mental focus and harnesses the power of your other-than-conscious. Crystal-clear concentration under pressure is the secret of success of all the great pros."* I also agree when he continues, *"The remarkable thing is that even though most golfers acknowledge that the game of golf is mainly a mental game almost no one does anything to improve their mental focus."* He even goes on to say some nice things about Milton Erickson – the father of modern hypnosis and the model for much of NLP as well.

So what am I uncomfortable with then? Well, it's his later suggestion that hypnosis can be used, and the implication that it should be used, in a negative way to somehow spoil your opponent's game. I disagree when he says that, *"It's great to use hypnosis to improve your own game, but some people take it farther and, let's say, 'help' the rest of the foursome by using hypnosis against them. When someone uses hypnosis this way, an opponent who's a superior golfer may find themselves somehow shanking the ball, having their drives slice into the rough, making poor club choices, deciding to try to drive the green when they shouldn't, or making any number of other such mistakes."*

I'm even more uncomfortable when he goes on to suggest that, *"It's up to you to decide the right and wrong of this, but a certain type of hypnosis does give someone the tools to influence their opponent's state of mind in addition to their decisions. Some say 'All's fair in love and war'. Maybe that's true in golf as well."* For me this suggestion goes totally contrary to the spirit of golf and is no different from suggesting that you actively seek to use hypnosis to distract or disturb your opponent's play. Apart from any moral consideration, that sort of behaviour is outlawed by Section 1 of the Rules of Golf.

Is there any truth in it?

Unfortunately there is some truth in it and a lot of the work clinical hypnotherapists do is involved in helping their clients to find ways to change and overcome unhelpful negative suggestions like the one's he proposes. So many of these clients have suffered for years, following unhelpful suggestions they received during vulnerable times in their past. Now while a very small number of these problems were caused by deliberate covert hypnosis, the vast majority happen through the careless, insensitive and unhelpful comments made by people in authority to vulnerable individuals.

I have successfully helped a number of people who have a deep fear of speaking in public. In most of these cases, the problems stem from their being called out in front of the class by an insensitive school teacher and forced to read out their poor homework, or perhaps explain the solution to a problem they don't understand. What's worse is that, while they are standing there feeling scared, embarrassed and shy, the teacher then scolds them, saying something like "you'll never speak in public" or "you'll never be a success in life". How many children who would love to have learned music or art were put off in a similar way? I struggled for years to write anything at all, because of a teacher telling me, "You'll never write!" when I was in tears while being forced to read out my poor essay in front of the class, as a punishment. Fortunately, I learned about hypnosis with a friend and now I'm writing articles, newsletters and this book.

At a more mundane level, we often say unfortunate things to children like, "don't spill your drink". With adults it may be something like the sales manager saying something like, "don't come back without the order" to his junior salesperson. Unfortunately, the mind has to think of doing something in order to think of not doing it. If I tell you "don't think of an elephant painted blue", it's almost impossible not to think of one, isn't it. In addition, your unconscious mind, like any other computing device, can only do the things you instruct it to do and it doesn't know how to not do something. So what happens, the child might be so nervous not to spill her drink that she does spill it and the salesman might be so nervous about not failing to win the order that he fails. And the child learns that she's prone to spill drinks and the junior salesperson learns that she's not good at selling. And the cycle continues.

You don't want to hit it in the bunker

So what's all this got to do with golf? Well, if you say to your opponent something like, "you don't want to hit your ball into that left-hand bunker, it's really difficult to get a par from there", guess what happens. Yes, you more often than not end up thinking consciously about the bunker when you play the shot and that's where the ball goes. Your opponent could be more subtle and say something like "you're new to this course, so I ought to tell you about that left-hand bunker..." He could be even more devious and say something like, "will you look at the swing of that player over there... the one behind that difficult bunker on the left" Or he could be both subtle and devious and say "you know, I went in that left-hand bunker the other week and it took me 3 shots to get out." Whichever one he says, you can guarantee the result will be the same.

I've used fairly extreme examples to illustrate the point I'm making and there are many other ways to use negative golf psychology against your clients, but I'm not going to reveal them all here, because I would never use them myself and I don't think you should either.

Anchoring other people and negative anchors

You learned back in Chapter 3, *NLP Anchoring for Better Golf*, about how to use techniques like the Finger-Thumb and *Circle of Excellence* to anchor positive resources to sensory experiences.

Well, anchoring can be used covertly against you and it can be used to anchor negative experiences and resources. Let's say we play golf together and every time you hit a good shot and are feeling great, I pat you on the back and say, "you're a great golfer". After a few repetitions, all I have to do, to put you in the right state to hit a good shot, is to pat you on the back and say "you're a great golfer", in the same tonality. Watch and listen carefully and you'll see some of the PGA Tour caddies positively using similar physical and verbal anchors with their players at crucial moments.

If you've seen Paul McKenna in action when he's giving a course, he does a lot of anchoring of key learning points by snapping his fingers and saying an anchoring phrase like "Now!" emphatically at the same time.

So what if someone was to anchor your bad shots in a similar way? He could put his hand on your shoulder and say something like "so unlucky", whenever you hit a poor shot to anchor your negative feelings. Later, when you were about to start your pre-shot routine for a critical shot, he could say "let's hope you won't be...so unlucky" and put his hand on your shoulder in the pause. It would be difficult to be in a good state of mind for that shot!

Lee Westwood's "Secret Plan" in Dubai

Lee Westwood and Rory McIlroy were playing amazing golf at the 2009 Dubai World Championships, the finale of the European Tour. However, their phenomenal play took second place for me, given the extreme golf psychology and covert golf hypnosis flying about.

First there was Lee Westwood's much talked about "Secret Plan". When the dust settled he admitted, *"Okay, if you really want to know, the secret was making everyone else think I had a secret, when I didn't really have one."* He had the rest of the field nervously waiting to find out what the plan was and, as a result, not concentrating on their own plans. Although I'm not comfortable with all this covert psychology, I have to admit that Lee's approach isn't that much different from Jack Nicklaus taking a positive psychological mindset out of his fellow competitors' complaints about the conditions, as I described in Chapter 5, *Winning Golf.*

Then there was the Lee's personal success story of how he regained his form when he explained that. *"The reason for the big turnaround in my confidence and stuff like that was catching my caddie, Billy Foster, at the beach party on Tuesday evening when he probably had enough Heineken to tell me what he really thought."* Lee went on saying, *"He said I'd not been myself recently. I'd paid too much attention to other people around me. He told me I'd been out here 16 years, which is longer than all three of them (McIlroy, Ross Fisher and Martin Kaymer) put together and have won 30 tournaments, which is more than they've all won. You've got to bully them on the golf course. You've got to be yourself again and get back to the instinct you had in the late 90s."*

I suspect that Billy's comments had a much more positive golf psychology impact on Lee than any negative one his "Secret" had on his opponents. Having said that, his anticipation of the disadvantage his "Secret" would have on them would clearly help improve his own state of confidence. He certainly seemed to think it had a detrimental effect on Rory McIlroy.

That leads me nicely on to Rory's apparent golf psychology disaster after playing with Lee in the first round at Dubai. Whatever impact that had on his game, it was his putting that let him down – if you consider coming third at Dubai and second in the Order of Merit a let-down. In contrast, it was Lee's phenomenal putting that made the difference between him and Rory and that was what really sealed his victory.

So if you want to play your best golf, you need to increase your psychological strength and confidence with golf hypnosis and protect yourself from covert hypnosis and other people's "Secret Plans".

Unintentional Distractions and Suggestions

Just as some people will deliberately point hazards out to you as a form of gamesmanship to distract you, others will do it inadvertently and with the best of intentions. Frustratingly the effect is the same. In fact, it's possibly worse, because if you come to expect the underhand comments from certain types of golfer's, it can throw you completely when someone is really trying to help you in a misguided way.

The same can happen when someone points out something that's worrying them and unwittingly shares it with you. If you're not careful, you end sharing in their fears and phobias. However, if you're competing against them, you're better to follow Jack Nicklaus and feed off their negativity, as I describe in Chapter 5, *Winning Golf*.

The Rules Official or Unofficial

If you play on the European Tour and in the majors, then you may well occasionally get distracted by the well intentioned interventions of the rules official. If you just play golf as an amateur, then it's more likely to be the interfering and sometimes ill-intentioned interventions of the self-appointed rules "unofficial". Either way, it can be bad news for your ongoing concentration, as Padraig Harrington experienced when John Paramor reminded him of the time pressures on the fateful 16th hole on the final day of the 2009 World Golf Championships at Firestone. Now I'm not saying that Tiger wouldn't have overhauled him and beaten him anyway, but Padraig certainly appeared to rush his next few shots with disastrous results. I'm sure that a scrupulously fair man like John Paramor had definitely not intended to make that happen.

Playing with a gallery – friendly or hostile

My first experience of playing in front of a gallery was terrifying despite the people being friendly and supportive, I just wasn't expecting to be watched and I was nervous enough as it was. That was a long time ago and well before I knew anything about golf psychology. If it happened now, I'd be better equipped to handle it and I could certainly have used the finger-thumb resource anchor to handle it better. If I was expecting it, I would probably use the *Six Steps to Mirroring Your Own Gallery* technique I described in Chapter 4, *Enjoying your Golf*, and put my own friendly face on the gallery.

I've never experienced playing in front of the huge galleries that follow the top professionals and I'm generally impressed with the way they handle the pressure. I'm sure that it's a distraction for the top flight players, but they surely want to get used to it. The people I feel sympathy for are the lesser players who occasionally get paired with a superstar and often have to play their shots while the gallery is hollering and rushing after their hero. Having said that, it is part of the challenge of the game at that level and it can be managed and overcome using straightforward golf psychology techniques.

Beware the Sick Golfer!

Have you ever had one of those days when you played better golf than normal, despite having your mind clearly focussed somewhere other than golf. Maybe it's when there's something exciting or absorbing going on in your life that has nothing to do with golf. At the other extreme, it could be a time when you're feeling ill or worried about yourself. I'm sure you've heard the expression, "beware the sick golfer" and that's what was said about YE Yang when he shot a 7-under par 65 on the Friday of the 2009 Chevron World Challenge at Sherwood Country Club. Afterward, he related the experience to what happened at qualifying school in 2008 when *"I had a huge headache because I was under a lot of mental stress."* This time, he went on, *"I still have a headache, but it's more because of illness, not because of any pressure or stress."* Another good example was Tiger Woods winning the 2008 US Open despite the obvious post-operative pain from his knee.

I know this isn't strictly Covert Hypnosis, but it is something to be aware of if you're playing a sick or distracted golfer. So don't assume that you'll win just because your opponent seems a little unwell.

So what's happening here? Well, if your mind is focussed elsewhere, it's your conscious mind that's doing the focussing, whether it's worrying about your health, doubting whether you should be out here on the golf course or just thinking about what you'll be doing after the game. The only part of you that's free to think about golf is your unconscious golf mind and trusting your unconscious is one of the most important and effective of the secrets of hypnotic golf.

Now, one of the keys to successful hypnosis and hypnotherapy is to pre-occupy or confuse the client's conscious mind, or simply send it off somewhere nice, while I communicate directly with her unconscious mind, the storehouse of all her knowledge, experience, skill and resources. Coming full circle, that's just what we're looking for when we're on the golf course and looking to trust our unconscious golf mind.

That reminds me of a story about the advice that Bob Rotella was giving Mike Weir before an important tournament recently. Any advice from Bob is usually good advice and what he told Mike Weir was to, *"Try to go unconscious on the course."* I looked that story up on the internet and found Bob saying pretty much the same thing about avoiding choking under pressure by turning off your conscious mind and switching to your unconscious one. He also tells his clients to, *"practice their swing technique all they want on the driving range, but on the course, let instinct take over."*

I agree that given an absolute choice between playing golf in the conscious or unconscious minds, I'd have to choose the unconscious for better golf. However, I think that the best golf is played using the conscious and unconscious golf minds selectively and independently for different tasks. There's an important separation in the mind between planning a shot, a conscious process, and executing it, an unconscious process. Have you noticed how when you hit a really good shot, you tend to think," Wow, what happened there? What did I just do right?" The odd thing is that it usually happens when you didn't have a thought, at least a conscious one, in your head.

Now isn't that more or less the same thing that happens when a golfer's conscious mind is "clogged up" with a cold or flu?

Take care listening to negative TV golf commentators

How much do you listen to the commentators on televised golf? Well, I used to think that watching golf on TV was good golf psychology. Now I'm less sure after watching a replay of the television coverage of the 2009 World Cup from Mission Hills in China. Now, I'm always thinking very positively when I watch golf, so I was amazed at how quickly I felt my negativity increasing the longer I listened to the commentators. Here is a selection of the negative comments I noted in just 30 minutes of watching and listening:

- *"He's got to think about trying not to let his partner down*
- *Very few golfers have found winning easy*
- *The nap is into him as well as the slope – he has to hit it hard*
- *Perhaps he was afraid of thinning it*
- *They might have felt a bit intimidated*
- *It's not finished yet*
- *It's only a par, but it's not terminal*
- *He missed one of this length at the last hole*
- *There's a tough driving hole coming up*
- *He'll be disappointed to be much farther away from the hole in 2 shots*
- *He and his playing partner have it all to do*
- *I still wouldn't like to call it, would you? No.*
- *For the third hole in a row he gets just this length of putt*
- *He's just 20 years old, what can you expect?*
- *Had that gone in, there might have been a glimmer of hope, but they are running out of holes"*

It makes depressing reading doesn't it? More worryingly, I wonder how many of those negative suggestions have been taken in by my unconscious and processed against my map of reality while I was watching and listening. I dread to think how depressing and potentially bad for your golf it would be playing with some of those commentators, if they talk like that when they actually play golf.

I'm not saying that television golf commentators don't ever say anything positive. You only have to hear them talking about their favourite player to hear them talking positively, even when he's playing badly. To be fair, some of the commentators are very positive, particularly the one's who played golf at the very top, like Nick Faldo, Johnny Miller and Peter Alliss – unless he's talking about putting!

So, be careful when you watch golf on TV. Enjoy watching the golf, learn from your favourite golfers and consciously filter out the negative comments from the positive commentary.

Part 4

The Secrets of Homework for Better Golf

Chapter 19

Analysing and Reviewing your Golf

"The best thing about the past is that it's over. The best thing about the future is that it's yet to come. The best thing about the present is that it's here now."
– Richard Bandler, creator of NLP

Traditionally, it seems that a lot of regular amateur golfers walk off the course muttering to themselves about all the bad shots they hit during the round and all the bad luck they experienced out there. When they get to the locker room, they start telling anyone who'll listen about their tale of woe, even if they scored well. This negative train of conversation will continue as they progress to the bar and reminisce with their playing partners and anyone else who'll listen. They will often regurgitate it all again when they get home and possibly when they get to the office on Monday morning. How many times have you heard someone come in with a good round and say things like, "it could have been even better if I hadn't three-putted the 15th green", "if only I hadn't driven so badly" or "I was so unlucky on the 5th hole". What message do their friends and more importantly their unconscious minds hear?

The better golfer may be more objective about things and reserve his judgement of the round until he's got home and analysed it fully. I know that's what I used to do before I learned better. I built this really complex spreadsheet and typed in details of my score per hole, the number of putts, chips, greenside bunker shots, greens in regulation and fairways hit. I also recorded what club I used, the type of shot, how well I hit the ball and whether it was long, short, left or right for every shot and every putt. It all got so complicated to remember that for a while I used to take a digital voice recorder in my pocket and record whispered details of every shot I played. What a nerd!

Once I'd entered in all the data, I'd designed my spreadsheet to automatically regurgitate information about my percentage accuracy and consistency for each of my clubs and each hole of the course for the current round and on average for the year. Even when I was playing my best rounds off a handicap of 2, the results were usually depressing and confusing. I didn't know back then that they were also harming my unconscious self-image and my golfing confidence.

So what about the top professionals? Well, the nearest we usually get to their thoughts about their golf is from the post-round interviews they give. Have you noticed how positive the regular winners on tour tend to be when talking about their rounds? They talk about the birdie here, the eagle there and the amazing recovery they made somewhere else. If they are pushed to answer a question about a bad hole, they talk in a very detached way about it. It's almost seems that they are describing what happened to someone else. Most importantly, they nearly always end the interview with a positive comment about their game.

So when you come in from a round of golf, tell everyone who wants to know about the good shots you hit and your lucky breaks. And if they remind you of a bad shot or bad break, talk about it in a detached way, almost as if it had happened to someone else.

Technique: Write down your Best Shots to Remember

You've finished your round, had the opportunity to relax a bit and now you want to see what you can learn from your round. I'm assuming here that you've either returned home, got back to the hotel or you're just relaxing in a quiet place for a few moments. Now thinking only about your good shots and experiences, think generally about the positives you can take from the round, recall your better shots in your mind and select the best six.

You can include shots that you hit just as you planned, even if they didn't hit the target. Alternatively, it could be shots that weren't absolutely perfectly struck that ended up close. You can also include shots that you planned to perfection. Go for a mixture of shots rather than just those six perfect drives you hit. There's no benefit at all from thinking about your bad shots and ill luck. If you were using a good post-shot routine, you'll have already learned what you can from those and released them to the past where they can't hurt you.

Now, just relax comfortably for a few minutes knowing you're in a safe, comfortable and quiet place. You can help your relaxation with a simple self-hypnosis technique, such as *Finger Breathing* from Chapter 2, *Hypnosis and Self-Hypnosis for Golf*. Now think about each of your best six shots from the round in turn and vividly recall what you saw, what you heard and, most importantly, what you were feeling at the time. Make the pictures larger, brighter and bolder and see all the action. Make the sounds louder and notice where they are coming from and really notice your external and internal feelings, maybe warmth or cold, the stillness or breeze and especially how good you felt. If you use an NLP resource anchoring technique, such as the finger-thumb or *Circle of Excellence* ones from Chapter 3, *NLP Anchoring for Better Golf*, now's the time to anchor it as a resource, while you're feeling just so good about that shot.

As soon as you've anchored the feeling, write a paragraph or two in your journal that describes that shot and the really great feeling it gives you. Now repeat that process for the other five shots and you're done. If you work with a golf-psychologist, a golf coach, a mentor or golfing friend, then tell them about what you've written or send them a copy. It'll make the experience even more profoundly beneficial.

Remember to review your journal from time to time, especially before an important game of golf, to remind you about your best shots and the wonderful way they make you feel.

The dangers of technically perfect golf

As I mentioned earlier, I used to analyse every shot I ever hit on the course to identify where I had to focus my efforts. All I achieved was to identify and focus on the parts of my game that needed improvement. I felt that I needed to be as near perfect as possible in every area of the game.

What I failed to notice was that the leading players, who are winning events on professional golf tours around the world, aren't always technically or statistically the best players. They have weaknesses as well as strengths and that means they often don't even look like the best player over the four rounds of the tournament the week they win. Now, I know that's a contradiction, because if they win the event, then they must be the best in that event.

Going back to the 2009 Masters, no one would suggest that Kenny Perry, Angel Cabrera and Chad Campbell were the best players in the field, but they were the one's that got into the playoff, despite their obvious mistakes. Many of the technically and statistically better players looked to be playing really well, but despite some amazing heroics from the likes of Phil Mickelson and Tiger Woods, none of them came near getting into the playoff.

You're often hearing me talk about how I started my golf during the golden years of my golfing hero Jack Nicklaus, the Golden Bear. Listening to me and many other pundits, you'd imagine that Jack was the most technically and statistically perfect golfer of all time. However, I have to admit that although he may still be the best golfer the world's ever known, he was physically and technically way behind the likes of Tiger Woods.

I recently picked up my rather well thumbed copy of Dave Pelz's Short Game Bible, published in 1999, and re-read his section on the ideal composite golfer. These were the players he scientifically picked as the top three golfers in each of six key technical areas. Interestingly, Tiger Woods appears only once as number two behind Greg Norman in Driving and Fairway Woods and Jack Nicklaus doesn't appear at all!

A more recent article broadly confirms these results, but this time it includes ratings for the Mental Game and Course Management. The truly great golfers, like Jack Nicklaus, Tiger Woods, Lee Trevino and Nick Faldo, rise to the top in these categories and demonstrate how they make the best of their all-round technical skills through their strength in the areas of golf psychology.

In conclusion, I suggest that although it's good to be as technically and physically competent as you possibly can, you're more likely to achieve consistently good golf by mastering the mental side of golf and focussing on how well you normally play the shot facing you, rather than how badly.

The dangers of analysis paralysis

Now you understand the risk of over-analysing your rounds of golf and the results for the various types of shots you play, what other dangers are there from analysis paralysis? Well, you could be tempted to want to know every technical detail of your swing with the various types of shot you hit and with your putting stroke.

Now that's no bad thing when you're on the practice ground and working on your swing, but concentrating consciously on how you swing when you're out on the course will generally prevent you from playing your best and most natural game of golf. There's a place for thinking consciously on the golf course and that's when you're planning where you want the ball to go and how you want it to get there. When you're hitting the shot, trust your unconscious mind to put your best swing to work, without any interference from the conscious mind.

I've heard over the years and read in some of the older golf books in my library about Ralph Guldahl, a really great golfer from the 1930s. After a relatively slow start as a professional golfer, he ended up winning 16 PGA Tour events in a nine-year period. He peaked with three Major wins toward the end of the 30s, but never won again after 1940. His Major wins were at the US Open at Oakland Hills in 1937, the US Open again at Cherry Hills the next year and finally the Masters in 1939. What's always seemed odd to me is that until recently, I've never come across anything about his record after that time. I guess that I thought he had died or been injured in the Second World War. Or perhaps, in a similar way to many great British golfers of the late 1930s, he never got back into winning again when professional golf competitions started up again after the war years.

The Secrets of Hypnotic Golf

So imagine my surprise when I came across an old news article that confirmed he had continued to play professional golf in the 1940s before becoming a successful club professional. The article went on to say that he had completely lost his game after taking a couple of months off in 1939 to work on his book *Groove Your Golf*. He started to struggle after that and never won again after 1940. Paul Runyan, twice US PGA Champion, said of him, *"It's the most ridiculous thing, really. He went from being temporarily the absolute best player in the world to one who couldn't play at all."*

So what happened? Well according to his wife, he went into such detail analyzing his swing, in order to write the book, that he could never play his natural game again. Others spoke of him practicing shots in front of a mirror, so that he could describe his exact movements in the book.

It certainly seems to me that, up to the time he was commissioned to write the book, Ralph Guldahl played with a natural free-flowing swing that he had learned unconsciously. Other articles I've read suggest that he was very relaxed on the golf course and just took a few moments to plan his shot before hitting the ball. Until he started analyzing his swing for the book, he probably had never even consciously thought about how he swung the club while he was on the course. In fact, it seems that everybody described him as a natural gifted golfer.

So if you want to play your best golf on the course, leave your swing thoughts on the practice ground, use your conscious mind to assess the shot and then trust your unconscious free-flowing swing to hit the ball.

Chapter 20

Better Golf with Less Practice

"They say practice makes perfect. Of course, it doesn't. For the vast majority of golfers it merely consolidates imperfection." – Henry Longhurst

You've probably been told for all your golfing life that the only way to better golf is practice, practice and more practice. I remember when I started out in golf in the 1960's hearing Gary Player responding to Henry Longhurst's suggestion about his luck in a tournament. Gary's response, in a clipped South African accent, was, *"Yes, Mr Longhurst. And the more and harder I practice, the luckier I get."*

You get the same response today from Vijay Singh, one of the hardest practisers in the professional game. He told Golf Today that, *"The secret is in the dirt – Golf is a job for me. I love to play, but I'm very serious about what I do. I don't think there is any excuse for me to play without being completely prepared, and that means practising until I'm confident and ready. That could be three hours and 300 balls even after I've played. The harder I work in practice and in the gym, the better my results are, so I'm not going to stop."* Doesn't that sound a lot like Ben Hogan talking?

The "best" advice anyone of my generation could receive was, find yourself a good teaching pro and have regular lessons – for the rest of your life. Next go down to the practice ground and practice each individual movement that the pro just taught you and repeat it until it becomes habit and you have a repeating swing. In other words, your best golf swing is buried in the practice ground. All you have to do is dig it out of the ground. And there's lots of pseudo-science out there to suggest that you need to practice each move 10,000 times and never change any part of it. Have these people thought out the practicalities of that? Have the people who regularly change their swings, like Padraig Harrington, Nick Faldo and Tiger Woods, done 10,000 identical repetitions for each element of each major or minor swing change? The problem for me is that if I practice long enough and hard enough, I can get more or less any swing to work, eventually. What's worse is that it's not usually there the day after I think I've mastered it, so it's back to square one again.

Let's look at Tiger's Practice Routine

While researching this part of the book, I asked myself the question, "just how much do people like Tiger have to practice to be as good as they are?" I fairly soon found the answer in a report from Hank Haney, Tiger's swing coach at the time. Here's how Hank described a typical day for Tiger between tournaments. Is it any surprise that he's starting to experience wear and tear to his body, at the young age of 33?

Time	Activity
06:00-07:30	Lifting weights in the Gym
07:30-09:00	Breakfast
09:00-11:00	Hitting balls on the range
11:00-11:30	Putting practice
11:30-12:30	Playing 9 holes of golf
12:30-13:00	Lunch
13:00-15:00	Hitting more balls on the range
15:00-16:00	Working on his short game
16:00-17:00	Play another 9 holes of golf
17:00-17:30	Hitting yet more balls on the range
17:30-18:00	More putting practice

Excuse me for a moment; I have to lie down to recover after just reading this!

Now I'm not saying that practice doesn't work at all. It clearly does, especially if you know you're practicing what the pro wants.

Better Golf with Less Practice

We can all hit good shots during a golf lesson, can't we? The problem is that when the pro's not there, the swing goes with him and we are left practising a suspect technique and ingraining our bad habits. What makes it worse psychologically is that without the pro watching us, we're often not sure if we're doing the right things.

Just how low could you go?

So where does that leave us? We all want to improve our golf, so what do we do? Well, it's all a matter of perception. For example, what would you say your personal lowest possible score is? What score should you be targeting when you play?

If you play off 10 handicap and you target shooting a couple of shots below that – that's an 80 round a par 72 course, isn't it. But that's nothing like the best you can perform. Let's say that your lowest ever was 6 shots below that level for a round of 74 – you must be a bit of a bandit eh! However, could you conceivably score better than that? Let's look at it from a different perspective. What I'm looking for is your potential, not your lowest actual score to date.

One way to find out how well you can score with your existing unconscious golf swing is to add up the lowest number of shots you've ever scored on each hole – your eclectic score. Ideally assess your scores on a course you play regularly. Now to add some reality to it, forget about any hole-score that included holing a full shot, chip or bunker shot, unless that's a part of your regular game! I've just done that and I'm astounded to find out that my eclectic score around Beaconsfield's par 71 adds up to 50, even after adding 3 shots to allow for the rather improbable eagles I'd scored on par 4's – as a result of holing long approach shots or driving the green. So, even if on average I play one shot above my best on every hole, I should still go round in 68 on average – 3 under par! I think I can cope with that, although my friends will struggle with the permanent silly grin on my face.

So given that I have the capability of scoring that well, why is it that whenever I used to have a bad round, I'd head for the practice ground to find out what was wrong with my swing or visit yet another golf guru to try and change it? I'm sure that sounds like many of the golfers you know as well. If a similar capability exists in your unconscious resources, why not access it through your mind with golf hypnosis rather than just learning to swing the club again. You already have a blueprint for a great golf game, why not follow it rather than tear it up and start again?

If you look at the annual saga of swing changes from three-time major winner, Padraig Harrington, you'll know that the same thing occurs with the very best golfers. That said, Padraig tends to change his swing when he seems, to the rest of us, to be playing his best golf ever, rather than after a bad round! He had a major overhaul of his swing at the end of 2008 after winning two Open Championships and one US PGA Championship in the previous 18 months! I read recently that he justifies this by saying that it's in his nature to seek to improve his swing every year. He backs this up by saying, *"The reason I improve is I actually stop and start rebuilding every year and change things. I think guys who stay constant are on a slippery slope to retirement. It's all about pushing yourself to get better."*

Now unless you have the consistency and are approaching the level of success regularly achieved by Padraig Harrington, I suggest that you focus using your golf mind on getting the best out of the swing you already have. There's no harm in seeing your regular golf instructor, if you need to, to make sure you haven't slipped into bad habits. Remember that the destructive shots you hit are more likely to come from your conscious thoughts than from your unconscious golf swing.

What do you believe is stopping you?

The world is full of self-perceived limits that stop us from being as good as we really are. At one time, people said it would be impossible for man to travel to the moon, to fly in airplanes or to watch moving pictures at home. The same thing applies in sports and people genuinely saw barriers like the 300 yard drive and the four minute mile. When Dick Fosbury decided to perform the high-jump with his back to the bar, the "Fosbury Flop", and set new records at the 1968 Olympics, they still said it was impossible and that he would break his neck doing it! People used to say there was no point in even manufacturing a 60 degree lob wedge and then Phil Mickleson came along. He didn't stop there and now uses a 64 degree one as well. I've got one and I know it works in certain circumstances on particular courses, but I still feel I'm in danger of hitting my face with the ball when I use it! So dare to go beyond your current limits and dare to set a course for improvement and stick with it. It needn't be as impossible or improbable as you may think.

I know that all this sounds a bit extreme, but the same sort of thinking applies to any other sport or business for that matter. You see, we are the sum of our experiences and our history. We tend to see and live in the future in just the same way we experienced the past. We know that many, many golfers have improved their game following the standard method of continuous change backed up with practice, practice and more practice. I've seen so many people do it and for many years I did it myself. What's more, there's a whole industry helping us do it. There are books, ebooks, websites, CDs, DVDs and magazines filled with more and more swing techniques, thoughts and ideas to fuel your quest for the perfect golf swing.

So you end up with a head full of conflicting thoughts that have little or no alignment with your unconscious golfing ability. That almost inevitably leads to a conscious confusion referred to as "Analysis Paralysis".

Analysis Paralysis and Golf Success

You do not improve your swing and achieve golfing success through analysis paralysis. People who teach complex swing thoughts just clutter the conscious mind and block out the unconscious mental processes that already know how to swing the club to the best of a player's ability.

Now don't get me wrong about the general standard of teaching from PGA golf professionals. It's truly magnificent and in nearly all cases their swing coaching advice is well thought out, simple, elegant and tailored to the golfer in front of them.

So what am I griping about, you may ask? Well, unfortunately the coaching advice available from the many websites, magazines, recordings and books is often over-complicated and, of necessity, far too generalised. Face-to-face with a golfer, a good pro will identify perhaps one or two key things for that golfer to work on at any one time. The author of a book or article, on the other hand, has little or no information about the individual golfing reader and therefore has to generalise. Now, that might be ok if the author has only one or two key points to get across and that's the only author the golfer is currently following. More than one or two swing thoughts when you're practicing can rapidly lead to analysis paralysis and reverse any golf improvement you were hoping for.

To show you what I mean, here's a list of swing thoughts from a single article on a golf improvement website. Now, if this set of suggestions doesn't lead to analysis paralysis, I don't know what will! Let's hear what the author suggests you do:

- *"reduce the moment of inertia of your swing to get more distance for less input*
- *delay the hand release*
- *increase the swing torque*
- *reduce the moment of Inertia – a function of the size of the mass and the radius of the mass and it applies because the swing is a rotating entity.*
- *remember that the swing radius is determined by the angle of your hand cock*
- *keep your hands cocked longer in the downswing to allow you to accelerate your trunk turn at specific moments*
- *need to reset your tempo and timing*
- *eliminate muscle tension*
- *swing naturally and keep your hands quiet!"*

Just imagine what it would be like to be given a check list like that to follow when you're driving your car!

What about all the improvements in golf equipment?

We've all seen big technology improvements in recent years, haven't we? All those new materials, shafts, high bounce drivers, etc. And what about the latest developments in golf ball technology? They've improved in leaps and bounds, haven't they? And the courses are so much better and the greens truer.

And with the huge boom in golf following the success of Tiger Woods, more and more young people are coming into golf – my club has far more young low handicap players than ever. So with all this enthusiasm and technology, golfers must be playing better and better, mustn't they?

Well no, actually. Recent studies have shown that the average handicaps of both men and women golfers have remained broadly stable for the last 40 years. With all the technological improvement, we must be playing worse, despite all that practice. Maybe that's the reason for the current oversupply of golf courses – many clubs are advertising for new members right now. Maybe people are leaving golf in frustration at not getting better.

So here's the problem as I see it. We want to get better at golf. We look to those that are very good at golf and ask them how they did it. They tell us that they worked their socks off practicing their technique for countless hours. We logically conclude that's the way to go.

The only thing is, in golf and in some other sports as well, most of us shouldn't be asking the playing professional how he or she got to the top ranks. We should model them and install the parts we want from their behaviour model in ourselves.

Now, I am a qualified Clinical Hypnotherapist and a Master Practitioner of Neuro Linguistic Programming. And the major theme behind NLP is – you've guessed it – modelling how successful people do what they do. And what NLP tells us is that these successful people think differently compared to the average person in whatever sport or business we are talking about. They don't follow the way everybody else does things. If they did, they wouldn't be of special interest to us.

So how do you learn best?

Have you ever been on a long car journey and suddenly thought, "How did I get here?" You know you started out on the journey, but you can't recall what happened in between. Well, it's alright; you drove perfectly safely, assuming you kept your eyes open. When you learned how to drive, maybe years ago, it was very difficult with all those things to remember. Now it's just an automatic, unconscious process. You don't even have to think about how to drive, just where. I'm repeating myself here, because it's such a good example.

Something similar happened to you if you learned to ride a bike. How many years is it since you last rode one? It doesn't matter; you'll just do it automatically when you next get on one. So why doesn't the same thing happen with your golf swing, especially after all that practice you've put in over the years? I seem to remember that golf was a lot easier to learn initially than riding a bike. And you didn't fall off and hurt yourself.

Can we model how we learn once and then successfully ride a bike for a lifetime and apply this same principle to golf? Well yes we can. We just have to stop trying to learn to play and start playing. If you're an experienced driver, you don't think about how to drive when you're planning a journey now, do you?

So is this belief stuff all new then?

Yes and no! The NLP stuff is all relatively new – Richard Bandler and John Grinder developed it in the 1970's and it continues to develop. However the idea of better golf without practice is a lot older.

Alex J Morrison wrote his book *Better Golf Without Practice* in 1940 at the peak of his career. He was the greatest golf teacher of his day by far and had his own golf school in New York. He taught golf to many famous celebrities, including Bing Crosby and Bob Hope. Are any of you old enough to have seen Bing's wonderfully smooth and slow swing? It was effortless right through to his death, playing golf at the age of 73. Perhaps Morrison's greatest contribution to golf was coaching Charlie Nicklaus, father of golfing legend Jack Nicklaus.

Better Golf with Less Practice

Examples of Morrison's sage words from the book include

- *"Five minutes in an easy chair, mentally rehearsing the Morrison Keys, which afford you a successful swing, will improve your game more than weeks of hip-swivelling on the practice ground with a blank mind."*
- *"You can give the right kind of attention to the Keys by seeing them clearly with your brain."*
- *"Unfortunately, instead of lower scores, most players finish with lower spirits and higher figures. And for their failures they invariably resort to that old alibi – 'lack of practice.' This seems logical, for very few players have the time or inclination for long hours of practice. Let me assure you that this excuse will no longer hold. That 'no practice' alibi is through, finished."*

In the next chapter, you'll learn about *Practicing and Playing Golf in your* Mind. That's a very efficient way to practice more and spend less time physically practicing.

Chapter 21

Playing and Practicing Golf in your Mind

"Champions aren't made in gyms. Champions are made from something they have deep inside them: A desire, a dream, a vision. They have to have last-minute stamina, they have to be a little faster, they have to have the skill and the will. But the will must be stronger than the skill." – Muhammad Ali

Research shows that the act of "Imagining" yourself doing something fires up the identical parts of the brain that would be activated if you were actually doing it. So if you're imagining yourself playing golf, the neurons you're using in your brain are the very same ones that you're using when you're physically playing the game. Indeed, some of the actual muscles involved in playing a real shot are activated and make the same movements at a barely noticeable level. You really do "physically" practice your swing when you imagine hitting the ball and you have no reason to hit a bad shot when you're practicing and playing in your imagination.

One of my favourite stories about the power of imagination in golf comes from an American Major, James Nesmeth. He was an average golfer consistently scoring in the mid 90's, until he developed a unique way of improving his golf game. It came when he spent seven years in North Vietnam as a prisoner of war. During those tortuous years, Nesmeth lived in solitary confinement inside a prison cell that measured four and a half feet high and 5 feet long. To keep from losing all hope, he realized that he needed to do something to occupy his mind. So, every day he played 18 holes of golf in his mind. He imagined everything in vivid detail from the country club he was playing at, to the smell of freshly cut grass in the summertime. He would imagine the grip of the clubs and practice his swing mentally many times until he perfected it. In reality, he had no place to go, so he spent four hours a day on the course in his mind never leaving any detail out. When he was released from prison and returned home, he played his first real game of golf for 7 years. He scored 74!

If all of that isn't enough for you, there are countless studies done on the effects of mental practice in sports. You see, it has now been scientifically proven that the brain and nervous system do not fully know the difference between real events and vividly imagined ones! So you can practice perfect golf in your mind and only have to hit balls to warm up or to play the game we all love.

Mental imagery works for medical students

Golfers and other athletes have regularly used mental imagery to complement their physical practice. Sometimes practicing golf in the mind actually produces better results than physical practice. In a study of medical students in Texas A&M University, groups of students were given 30 minutes of guided practice for a complex medical procedure followed by either

1. no further training
2. a further 30 minutes of physical practice
3. 30 minutes of guided mental imagery.

In follow up tests, the students who did the guided mental imagery performed at the same level as those who had the additional physical practice. And both these groups were significantly better than the group who received no further training. The researchers saw the same thing happening with students learning to suture.

Mental Rehearsal can be better than physical practice

According to studies at California State University – Northridge, mental rehearsal can be even better than physical practice, because it activates more abstract neural representations of physical skills. So if you practice a particular stroke with your

Playing and Practicing Golf in your Mind

teaching professional and then inadvertently practice it incorrectly when you're on your own, you may well be rehearsing the wrong movements and making it more difficult to relearn the correct ones later. Mentally practicing a clumsy shot is not, in muscular terms, detailed enough to hurt your swing. However, it is still detailed enough to help you learn and experience the correct movements.

There's even some research ongoing that's finding proof that when you mentally rehearse a physical action, your unconscious mind sends out messages to build up the muscles needed to perform the action.

Practicing and playing golf in your mind really does work and generates the appropriate muscle responses for whatever you're vividly imagining. It's not clear why, but the implication is that imagined performance really does exercise much of the brain's motor function. It isn't all imagination, after all.

So when you find yourself with nothing important to do, maybe when you're travelling on public transport, when there's nothing worth watching on television or you're just daydreaming, just go inside your golf mind and imagine playing a round of golf. You may be surprised by the positive results.

Playing golf in your imagination

The more you visualise and see yourself hitting good shots, the more you will build your confidence and your expectation of hitting great shots. Unconsciously, your mind doesn't really know the difference between a good shot you hit and a good shot you imagine, so I think you should take the opportunity to "play" rounds of golf in your mind. Imagine arriving at the ball for each shot in the round and going through your full pre-shot routine, including visualising the shot you want to hit. Then imagine taking a good rehearsal swing before stepping into the ball, checking your alignment, taking one last look at your target and starting your swing – just as soon as your eyes are back on the ball. The only thing you should be thinking about is your visualisation of the shot or putt you want to hit, as you trust your unconscious mind to swing the club.

In the same way as on the course, watch your shot or putt travel toward the target, just as you visualised it would, and learn from it. Finally, remember to watch the shot fly and/or roll to a finish. As you're playing in your imagination, it's a good shot, so savour it and consign it to your memory – just like you would a good shot on the course.

Remember that you can use this imaginary golf to prepare you for an important game. If it's a course you haven't played before or one you don't know that well, then get hold of a course planner and imagine playing the course from that. It would be even more powerful if you could see a video "fly-by" of each hole and services like those starting to spring up on the internet.

Also remember to visualise playing your imaginary golf in all your senses and really live the experience, seeing what you'd see, hearing what you'd hear and feeling what you'd feel both physically and emotionally. There's lots more information in Chapter 6, *The Power of Visualisation for Golf*, including the Seven Steps to Effective Visualisation and Sensory Recall.

Imagine your own overhead shots from Snoopy 1 and 2

Effective visualisation is one of the key golf psychology tools for improving your golf score and your enjoyment of the game. It's also one of the secrets of hypnotic golf. However, for most people, including me until recently, that visualisation tends to be two dimensional, a bit like looking through the viewfinder of a camera or at a picture on a television screen. Yes, I know that I could imagine some depth perspective, but what if I couldn't actually see the bottom of the pin over that high lip of the bunker at the front of the green. That meant that I was looking at the lip of the bunker in my minds eye and then having to mentally add some more for the distance between the lip and flag. That's too complicated for my golf mind!

I came up with the solution while watching a US PGA Tour event on television. I was probably half asleep at the time, as we see the US golf late in the evening here in the UK. Anyway, I was marvelling at how much more information I was getting from the overhead shots from the blimp, when I realised that they were

Playing and Practicing Golf in your Mind

helping me to build more of a 3-dimensional image of the shots I was seeing played. As often happens with television, we get to see more than we would if we were actually there. That's when I had a sudden flash of inspiration. Why not visualise all my shots in 3D by incorporating an imaginary overhead shot. It sounded difficult until I realised that if I can see it on TV, then surely I can visualise it. After all, I already had the overhead view on the course planner, so why couldn't I incorporate it in my pre-shot routine visualisation and mental golf practice.

So, later that evening I took myself into a light trance using self-hypnosis and played an imaginary round of golf at Beaconsfield, my home course. I visualised playing every hole and every shot in 3D, even the putts. It worked great and I couldn't wait to take the idea to the course. That Friday, I got the chance to use it in my pre-shot visualisation on the real course and it worked amazingly well. Initially I found that I got the best results from visualising the shot normally, as a picture in 2D, and then "seeing" it again as if from a blimp, just as I stepped into the shot. By the time I'd played a few holes, visualising the shot in 3D, it just became a natural part of my routine.

What surprised me most was that it gives me so much more confidence, especially when hitting over a hazard or trees to my target. Instead of seeing the trees or hazards and estimating how far to hit past them, I'm finding myself seeing the whole shot from above. I'm getting a much clearer idea of the shot I'm playing and that's taking away a lot of the doubt I normally have when playing these shots.

Imagine the trouble your partner got you into

Most of my clients regularly play rounds of golf in their mind, as an important part of their regular golf improvement programmes. However one or two used to tell me that, although they gained significant benefit from their imaginary rounds of golf, it could sometimes feel a bit "unreal", as they were always hitting the ball from the tees, fairways and greens. Not surprisingly, they didn't allow themselves to hit bad shots in their imagination, so how were they to experience recovery shots from the rough, around the green and bunkers.

Well, there is a better way. How about playing some of those imaginary rounds in golf hypnosis as foursomes, playing alternate shots with an imaginary partner? You could choose a partner who is a less than consistent player. It could be someone you know, who hits a lot of bad shots, or just an imaginary partner. That way you'll get to play all sorts of difficult shots, without taking any conscious or unconscious responsibility for the bad shots. After all, you didn't hit them, that partner of yours did. What's better is that you don't need to worry about his golf, as you'll never play with him in real life!

Play Better Golf in your Dreams

> *"Wednesday night I had a dream and it was about my golf swing. I was hitting them pretty good in the dream and all at once I realized I wasn't holding the club the way I've actually been holding it lately. I've been having trouble collapsing my right arm taking the club head away from the ball, but I was doing it perfectly in my sleep. So when I came to the course yesterday morning I tried it the way I did in my dream and it worked. I shot a sixty-eight yesterday and a sixty-five today."* – Jack Nicklaus

These words are from an interview with Jack Nicklaus in 1964, two years after he won the 1962 US Open at Oakmont in a playoff with Arnold Palmer. Jack had been in a serious slump, when one night he dreamed he was playing much better and noticed, in his dream, how he was holding the club the way he used to. He reverted back to his old grip and suddenly started playing well again.

This concept ties in well with the old idea of people saying "I'll sleep on it" when they had an intractable problem to solve. I've also heard people talk about coming up with new ideas in dreams. Sir Paul McCartney has spoken about how the tune for *Yesterday*, one of the most popular songs of all time, came to him in a dream.

Playing and Practicing Golf in your Mind

Dr Otto Loewi won the Nobel Prize for a breakthrough discovery in neuroscience that he claimed he discovered in a dream. Novelist Stephen King also says that the ideas for some of his novels come from his dreams. However impressive these dreams were, to the best of my knowledge none of them was planned, so how long do we have to wait for the right dream to come along?

Well that's where Lucid Dreaming in Hypnosis comes into its own. Hypnosis works by communicating with your unconscious mind. And your dreams, the ones you have when you sleep or daydream, are also the work of your unconscious mind. We all spend a lot of our time sleeping, so why not use some of that time to practice and improve your golf with lucid dreams.

Technique: Eight Steps to Practicing Golf in your Sleep

Lucid dreaming needs a bit of practice before you start getting significant results, but it's worth persevering. This is a self-hypnosis technique that works best when you direct your mind using self-talk and use your imagination to the full. Initially, you may struggle to not fall asleep during the process, because your unconscious mind associates dreaming with sleeping.

Prepare by finding a safe, comfortable and quiet place to sit or lie down, where you'll be free from any interruptions for a while. I tend to use this technique when I lie down at night. Make sure that your mobile and any other phones in the room are muted or simply turned off. Now, if you're familiar with self-hypnosis, use your preferred technique to take you into a nice relaxed trance state with a receptive and imaginative mind. Alternatively, you can achieve the same with either the *Finger Breathing* or the *Betty Erickson* self-hypnosis techniques included in Chapter 2, *Hypnosis and Self-Hypnosis for Golf.*

Step 1: Start by counting backwards from 300 to 200, with one count for each inhale and one for each exhale, as you breathe deeply and rhythmically in and out in time with your counting. Stay relaxed, natural, still and in the moment, as you tune in to counting the numbers down.

Step 2: Begin noticing a heaviness moving up from your toes into your feet. Imagine it as a colour, a sensation and even give it a sound, as you really sense the heaviness you feel in your mind moving slowly up through your legs, your upper body, and your arms and all the way up until you reach the top of your head. Use your self-talk to guide you through the process, as you imagine the feeling of being weighed down by gravity. Feel as if you had comfortably heavy weights attached to your limbs – pinning you down.

Step 3: Imagine taking this to another level, as a second wave of heaviness is enveloping you. Notice how the heaviness doubles down through your body, cell by cell and atom by atom, from the top of your head to the tips of your toes. Be sure to take as long as it takes or longer, while you're intrigued to notice an increasing sense of heaviness, with big sand bags, double the weight before, weighing down your shoulders, wrists, waist and ankles. Really engage in this absorbing mental process.

Step 4: Now, take some time to imagine a blackboard directly in front of you, with the entire alphabet written across the top and the numbers zero through to nine written underneath the letters. Notice how the 36 letters and numbers seem to be representing every golf instruction article, book, video, audio recording and lesson you've ever experienced. Now go through and erase each letter and then each number in order, while thinking repeatedly, "all this knowledge and instruction is of no consequence to me right now. It only matters when I'm dreaming and when I'm fully awake. However, all that matters right now is my goal to have regular, long, vivid, highly lucid, realistic dreams of playing golf with full conscious control and with complete recall of those dreams every time I awaken." You can add specific details of where you're playing, who you're playing with and what you want to experience. Fully expect to have lucid golfing dreams – create that expectation.

Step 5: Next, imagine a small aeroplane slowly flying overhead, as it writes your name really slowly with its smoke trail. Imagine it as vividly as you can and now, as the plane flies off, imagine your name just drifting away on the wind. Now use your self-talk to tell

Playing and Practicing Golf in your Mind

yourself, "Who I am is of no consequence right now. Who I am matters when I am dreaming and when I am fully awake. However, all that matters right now is my goal to have regular, long, vivid, highly lucid, realistic golfing dreams with full control and with complete conscious recall of the dreams every time I awaken." Add the same specific details you included in Step 4.

Step 6: In the same way as in Step 1, breathe in and out deeply, while counting down from 200 to 100. Tell yourself that with each number you count, you relax deeper and deeper. Imagine that you're drifting deeper inside your own mind.

Step 7: Once you have reached 100, give yourself the suggestion that, "From now on I have regular lucid golfing dreams, dreams that are long, vivid, realistic, under my complete control, and remembered when I awaken." Again, add any specific details you included in Step 4 and, as you deliver the message, embed it deeply within you as you complete this process.

Step 8: Now, wriggle your fingers, wriggle your toes, take a couple of deep, sharper breaths and open your eyes. Take as much time as necessary to really reorient with your surroundings. Afterward, you might want to fall asleep, or go about your business, whichever is appropriate. It is important here to consciously forget any desire for dreaming. You'll know when something happens, won't you now.

Chapter 22

Learn from your Golfing Heroes

"Atticus was right, you never really know a man until you stand in his shoes and walk around in them..."
– Harper Lee, To Kill a Mockingbird

There are techniques in NLP and Golf Hypnosis that can be used to metaphorically step into the shoes of someone you'd like to model or learn something from. Perhaps there's somebody that does something really well and you'd like to know how or why they do it. Tiger Woods comes to mind as a model for many aspiring golfers. Now there's nothing to stop you 'walking a mile' in Tiger's or any other role model's shoes – in your mind at least.

Remembering good shots from your past can help you to recover your lost swing feelings and, even if you can't fully remember an exact model shot from your past, you can still imagine one that you might have hit. Your unconscious has the ability to generalise your past experiences to do its best to recreate the shot you imagined. So why not imagine how your role model thinks, plans and executes each shot.

One way to do this is with an NLP technique that Richard Bandler rather dramatically describes as *"Stealing a Skill"*. It's a technique that you can use with or without hypnosis. I first learned it from Richard on an NLP Master Practitioner course in 2007 that he co-hosted with Paul McKenna and John LaValle.

So how well does it work? Well I first tried it during that course when I was paired with a very nice, very tall and very imposing young Sikh guy; you'll see why that's important later. We had been asked to identify a suitable role model, ideally a personal hero, who we'd like to *"steal a skill"* from or at least learn to understand better. We were reminded that it may be easier if our partner for the exercise also knew something about our role model.

By now, you probably won't be surprised to hear that I chose Jack Nicklaus, possibly the best golfer the world has ever seen and my childhood hero, as the person whose shoes I wanted to step into. Unfortunately, my young friend had no idea who Jack Nicklaus was and suggested I switch to Tiger Woods, who he had heard of. I agreed, although I have to admit that I was reluctant, as at that time I found Tiger to be rather arrogant on the golf course, at least from what I had read about him and seen for myself on television.

I then asked my partner about the shoes he wanted to step into. Imagine my shock when he mentioned Bruce Lee, the famous martial artist! Did I want to be close up to a six foot six inch Sikh warrior version of Bruce Lee? Thankfully, my partner became a very thoughtful Bruce Lee for the next fifteen minutes and learned a lot about his hero. I survived the encounter!

So what did I "steal" from Tiger Woods or learn about him? Well the experience was really illuminating and nothing like I had expected. By assuming Tiger's persona, based on what I had seen on television and read about in books, articles and on the web, I realised that his apparent arrogance on the course was more a slightly hypnotic and patient embarrassment.

Before, I'd seen a rather petulant haughtiness when I watched him waiting while marshals cleared a path for him or searched for his ball. Now I experienced a rather thoughtful young man, politely waiting, while other people got on with their jobs, and at the same time embarrassed by all the fuss they were making. I also realised that his "distance", from his playing partners and the enormous gallery, was just part of his self-hypnosis based approach to managing himself on the course. It was all very revealing and not at all what I had expected.

As Tiger is so much younger, lighter and fitter than I am, I chose not to attempt to learn from his swing. After all, I'm more

Learn from your Golfing Heroes

interested in the psychological aspects of his amazing golfing abilities.

Deep Trance Identification

If you want to use hypnosis to *"steal a skill"*, then the best known, and in my view the most effective, technique is Deep Trance Identification, where you learn to take on a complete set of skills for particular tasks performed exceptionally well by your role model. You need a good hypnotist to help you into a really profound hypnotic trance and then lead you to recollect everything that you have known, seen and imagined about your target person. The hypnotist will then help you to mentally "step in" to that person and guide you through the experience of their world, completely in your imagination. Your unconscious mind builds new understandings about the person without critical analysis from your conscious mind.

Having said that, the *Stealing a Skill* technique is still my favourite NLP method for this and it has the advantage that, although it may work better initially with the help of an NLP Practitioner, you can achieve a lot of success with it on your own.

Choose your Role Models Carefully

Although golf is largely a mental game, there's a large physical element to it, so you might want to choose a role model who has a similar physical stature to you, to get the most out of *Stealing a Skill*. If you're short and stocky, there might be something about the swing that suits you that doesn't suit someone who is tall and slender. It might be harder to relate your swing motion to theirs. However, if you have to choose between someone with a better swing, but a different physical build, then I would use the role model with the better swing.

Sometimes you can see the qualities you'd like to model in two different golfers, so bear in mind that you can just as easily imagine your ideal role model having a combination of skills from two or more different role models. Maybe one has a particular swing feature, but the wrong temperament. Maybe you'd like Tiger Woods without the bad language and with the short game of

Padraig Harrington, for example. Remember, you're only limited by your imagination, so that shouldn't limit you, now should it.

Technique: Seven Steps to Stealing a Golfing Skill

Step 1: Start by finding a safe, comfortable and quiet place to sit or lie down, where you'll be free from any interruptions for a while. Make sure that your mobile and any other phones in the room are muted or simply turned off.

Now, just take in a few deep breaths, while mentally focussing on a spot an inch or so below your belly button, known as the Hara. Feel that you're inhaling a wonderful sense of relaxation and notice how you're exhaling any stresses and strains of your day.

Alternatively, if you're familiar with self-hypnosis, then use your preferred technique to take you into a very light and relaxing hypnotic trance with a receptive and imaginative mind. You can achieve that with either the *Finger Breathing* or the *Betty Erickson* self-hypnosis techniques included in Chapter 2, *Hypnosis and Self-Hypnosis for Golf*.

Step 2: Decide on a role model – someone whose physical and mental golf performance you would like to replicate or learn from. Spend as much time as possible studying your role model in the flesh, on video recordings, on websites, in books and in your imagination. Simply relax while taking all this in, softening your vision and hearing, as you are experiencing the flow of your role model's golfing performance.

Step 3: When you feel as familiar as possible with your role model's golfing performance, close your eyes, relax and recreate your role model. Imagine your role model playing golf and forming a sequence of actions at the highest level of excellence. See and hear everything there is in your imagination to build a model of that competence.

Step 4: When you have watched this performance for some time, move around the mental image of your role model and step inside. Imagine that you're able to vividly see through the eyes of excellence, hear through the ears of excellence and experience the feelings of excellence. Amplify those feelings to make them larger, brighter and bolder than in real life.

Step 5: Run through the same sequence of actions but from within, noticing this time what your body feels as you do this. Repeat this step several times, as you build a sense of familiarity.

Step 6: After an appropriate amount of time, imagine yourself stepping out of your role model's body, with the intention of retaining as much of the skill as you could possibly need, as you return to normal waking consciousness.

Step 7: As soon as possible (and as much as possible) practice the borrowed skill on the golf course and in your rounds of golf, noticing how this improves your performance.

Repeat the entire exercise, combining it with whatever real time golf opportunities you have, at least once a day for the first 21 days, then at least once a week as you gain more and more skills from your role model.

Technique: "Playing" golf with your Heroes

How do you get effective competitive golf practice when you play golf on your own? This is a problem facing many of my clients. For a variety of perfectly good reasons, many of my clients play a lot of practice rounds on their own, perhaps grabbing a few holes when they get home from work or when they might otherwise be just raking balls on the driving range. Sometimes people find it embarrassing to play with someone else, for example when they are integrating a new swing idea from their golf pro or working on a golf psychology homework task, such as the one below.

So the next time you're out playing on your own, whether it's for a full round or just a few holes, try one of these homework tasks that I sometimes give my golf hypnosis clients.

1. If the club rules only allow you to play one ball, imagine you're playing as one of your golfing heroes. It could be anybody you like, Tiger Woods, Jack Nicklaus, Annika Sörenstam or perhaps just you, playing to the best of your capabilities. It's your choice. Take on all the mannerisms of

The Secrets of Hypnotic Golf

your role model, imagine how they would be thinking and what they would be seeing, hearing and feeling.

2. If you're allowed to play 2 balls around your course, then follow the instructions for the first homework task, but this time imagine you're playing as one role model for the first ball and a different one for the other. Keep score and see which "person" has the best score – you may learn something here. It could be interesting to play as Tiger Woods with one ball and Phil Mickelson with the other. Although I wouldn't recommend playing left handed if you normally play right handed!

If you're not really sure exactly who you want to model, then try modelling a number of different players or a composite one. Over a period of a couple of weeks, you should be able to identify the one who helps you the most.

There's also a way that you can play golf with or in the character of one of your heroes in your imagination and learn a lot from the experience. You can learn more about the benefits of playing golf in your imagination in Chapter 21, *Playing and Practicing Golf in your Mind*.

Appendix 1

Introduction to Golf Hypnosis

Before you first experience golf hypnosis and start using it to make wonderful, beneficial changes in your golf and your life, I would like to answer some of your possible questions and to dispel a few popular myths and misconceptions you may have about hypnosis.

One very common idea people have is that being in hypnosis is the same as being unconscious, but that wouldn't work, as I need to communicate with your subconscious or unconscious mind to help you achieve anything from hypnosis.

That wouldn't be possible if you were out cold!

My own first experience of hypnosis was one of being extremely relaxed and calm, but fully aware of what was going on round me. It was a large training course run by Paul McKenna with over 400 people in the room and we split into pairs or groups of three to practice hypnosis. The room was very crowded with assistants rushing about helping people. Then one of them accidentally rushed closed by and nearly knocked me right off my chair. I did not react in any way and just thought to myself, "that was odd" and continued to focus on what the hypnotist was saying to me. That certainly wasn't the way I'd react normally if that happened!

Conscious and Unconscious – Different Levels of Mind

The human mind operates on two levels, the conscious and the unconscious or subconscious. The conscious mind is where we spend most of our waking life. It's where we make everyday decisions and analyse things. The unconscious mind operates just below our level of consciousness and generally manages the things we do automatically, like breathing and digesting our food.

We may consciously decide to put on our shoes, but our unconscious ties the shoelaces – assuming it knows how to. Do you remember how difficult that was for a while when you were very young? That was when you were doing it consciously and thinking a lot about how to do it. You may remember the same problem learning to ride a bike, drive a car or swing a golf club.

You know what it feels like playing after you've recently had a golf lesson and you're consciously trying to remember all the things the Pro told you to remember. It probably went something like – , "head down, now take it back in one piece, not too fast, don't pronate your wrist too much, keep your weight on the right or left side…" It was amazing that you could still hit the ball. Now I know that not all Pros are like that.

The Conscious Mind – the four basics

Your conscious mind basically does four things.

Analysis Paralysis

First, your conscious mind analyses. What is that? Well that is the part of us that looks at problems, analyses them and tries to create solutions. It is that part of us that makes decisions all day every day: "shall I open the door", "Shall I have something to eat", "what shall I worry about" or "what club should I take here? Even though they seem to be automatic behaviours, we make a conscious decision about whether or not to do these things.

Rationalizing – Why did that happen?

The second thing our conscious mind does is to rationalize. This is the part of us that, especially in western cultures, always has to understand why – why things happen and why did I just do that. This can cause us so much trouble, as we give any problems more and more credence and power. More conventional and traditional methods of golf psychology coaching are often very much concerned with looking at the causes of our problems.

I feel that all this does is to teach us "why" the problems happen as opposed to giving us the skills we need to change unwanted habits and behaviours. The more we think about "why" we do things, the more we seem to embed the unwanted behaviour into our lives. Think of some of the things we hear people say, and maybe say quietly to ourselves, on the golf course. They ask, "Why did I slice the ball into the trees?" and then hook the next one – after trying to change their swing there and then.

Willpower and Determination

The third part of our conscious mind is willpower, that teeth gritted determination that so many of us are proud to demonstrate. How many times have we used our willpower alone to make changes and found that our resolve weakens and that change is temporary or nonexistent? We have willpower to overcome immediate problems, not long term ones. Have you noticed how difficult it is to remember to maintain your concentration for a full round of golf – no matter how hard you try.

Short Term Memory

The final part of our conscious mind is our short-term memory. By that I am referring to the things that you need to remember to function on a day-to-day basis, so that when your phone rings you know to answer it rather than stare at it, wondering what it is.

Put it all together and our conscious mind is logical, rational, analytical and focussed on the short-term, a bit like Mr Spock from Star Trek. Unfortunately, our conscious mind often over-analyses things and sometimes ends up with the wrong answer. I remember in my childhood that my first answer to an exam question was usually right. Then of course, I changed it after further thought and got the answer wrong! It's probably true about some of your decisions on the golf course. How many times do you quickly decide on the shot to play before changing your mind and mishitting the shot?

Your conscious mind is wherever you happen to be focussed on at the current time, but your unconscious mind is noting and recording everything it can hear, see, smell, taste or feel – all the time.

As an example, each of our eyes has something like 6 million direct connections to the brain with about 40 of them – the ones for the fovea – connected to the conscious mind, covering what we are currently focussing on. The remaining 5,990,960 are connected to the unconscious mind, covering your full peripheral vision.

The same goes for our other senses. I am sure you have been in a busy, noisy environment, such as a restaurant, bar or on the golf course, and have been engaged in a conversation with someone, and all the sounds going on around you just seem to blend into the background. Then suddenly someone else away in the distance can punctuate their sentence with your name and you pick it out as if it was being spoken to you.

If you take that conscious awareness and point it inside of yourself instead of outside into the world, you begin to become aware of your inner self, your unconscious mind, which is the part of you that we work with in hypnosis.

The Inner You: Your Unconscious Mind

Your unconscious mind is tremendously powerful and automates as much behaviour as it possibly can, so that we do not have to consciously think about it.

We are amazing learning machines and we learn behaviours and habits consciously and then our unconscious mind automates them and does them on autopilot so that we do not have to think about doing them.

Long Term Memory – Just about every blade of grass on every course

Your unconscious mind has within it all your long-term memory. Just about every blade of grass on every hole of every course that you have seen in playing your entire golfing life is stored away in your long-term memory ready for instant access given the right cue.

As an example, have ever seen a live stand up comedy show? You watch the comedian and hopefully laugh heartily as you listen to lots and lots of jokes. Then when you leave the venue, you can remember none of them, or one or two at best! Then, a week later, a friend that you were with can just start to tell one of the jokes and you instantly remember the whole joke. The joke was stored away in your unconscious mind, just needing the trigger to find it.

You may experience the same thing listening to one of your old music albums that you haven't played in a long time. I often can't remember the words until the track starts, but then I can sing along happily, even if you turned the music off. I also start singing the next track before the previous one has finished!

If that sounds confusing, just think, you're currently breathing, your heart is beating, you're digesting your last meal, and your mind/body is regulating your body temperature and many other things. Your unconscious mind is managing a whole range of wonderful things without you having to consciously think about it. You're not sitting around thinking "I really must remember to breathe".

Your Gut Feelings, Instincts and Intuition

Your unconscious mind is where you get your gut feelings, your instincts and your intuition that communicate with you sporadically from time to time. Like when someone is saying all the right words to you, but you get a different feeling about them.

Your unconscious mind is a bit like a computer. Throughout your entire lifetime it has programmed itself with every skill you have ever gained, all your experiences, relationships, interpretations of the world, influences and beliefs. All this has culminated in your computer functioning with that programming. Hypnosis is simply a way of accessing that computer and understanding and updating that programming, so that it becomes instinctive and intuitive for you to make the changes that please you.

Your unconscious mind is the seat of your emotions and where your behaviours exist. It is the part of you that we work with in hypnosis. Hypnosis is our way of stepping over your conscious mind and accessing your unconscious mind to make powerful and profound changes.

You've Experienced Natural Trance States Before

You may be surprised to hear that hypnosis is not new to you. I am sure that you have experienced natural trance states many times before; in fact I know you have. For example, when you have been driving in a car and thought to yourself "how did I get here?" or when you have been reading a thrilling book or watching an exciting film and found yourself completely absorbed and with your heart pounding. Have you ever seen someone watching a physical sport, like football or boxing, begin to move with the action? They are in a hypnotic trance.

If you're really lucky, you've experienced a trance state while playing golf – some people describe it as being "in the Zone". For most golfers, who only experience it once in a while, it manifests itself as a wonderful sense of calm, relaxed confidence. They seem to float along without any real thoughts in their heads. Unfortunately, it just seems to fade away as soon as they realise how well they are playing.

The only difference, between these naturally occurring states and those that we use in golf hypnosis, is that with hypnosis, you intend to enter the state, you're in control of it and it is just like an amplified, deeper version. It's simply like sitting in a chair relaxing with your eyes closed, not the magical, mystical or unreal experience that some people may lead you to believe it is. And you're always in control.

Does the Hypnotist have any Power over me?

It is important – very important – here to know that you cannot be made to do anything in hypnosis that you don't want to do or wouldn't normally do. If I ask you to stand up, you will probably do it. If I suggest you rob a bank, you wouldn't. Unless it's something you're used to doing and are comfortable to do again – on my say so!

But what about Stage Hypnosis?

What about stage hypnosis you may ask, where the hypnotist asks people to do things that they would not normally do? Or would they? I have observed that many people who get up on stage "to be hypnotised" are extroverts who want to be the life and soul of the party.

Typically a good stage hypnotist will select those people who want to be on the stage and then go through some sort of selection test to pick the ones that really want to perform. He'll also create an uninhibited atmosphere where everybody expects them to act in a silly manner.

I do not believe that the hypnotist makes the people on stage do anything they don't want to. In fact, I have seen someone come out of hypnosis during a stage hypnosis performance and explain afterward that he wasn't ethically comfortable with a particular task the hypnotist asked him to perform. Up to that point he was participating fully in the show.

And what if I don't come out of Hypnosis?

People are often concerned about what happens if I get stuck in a trance? The simple answer is that you can come out of trance any time you like, regardless of the hypnotist. It may be that you're so comfortable in trance that you may not want to come out immediately when the hypnotist asks you to. It's your choice when you come out.

What if I can't be Hypnotised?

Anyone can be hypnotised as long as they want to be, even insomniacs, drug addicts, schizophrenics, people experiencing chemotherapy and people who are convinced that they cannot relax or be hypnotised. They all can and they all do, if they want to.

All that is required is to have an open mind, expect it to work and have progressive, motivated thoughts about the processes.

Then listen to the hypnotist and allow him to help you to make the changes you want and deserve.

So what exactly happens when I'm in Hypnosis?

Finally, during an individual hypnosis session and in my hypnotic audio recordings, I may ask you to do a number of different, seemingly contradictory, things with your mind. You could be forgiven for thinking "What exactly am I supposed to be listening to and doing?" The simple answer is that you listen to and follow as much or as little as you want to. Remember, it's your conscious mind thinking those thoughts and that's not the part of your mind that we're working with and making the changes with.

I am sure that there will also be times when you'll be thinking "am I in hypnosis, what am I supposed to be thinking or feeling?" Again that is your conscious mind thinking that thought and it does not matter what it is thinking right now, just trust that your unconscious mind is absorbing all that you want it to.

There will be times in the sessions and recordings when I ask you to imagine things. Imagining things does not have to mean visualising. If I ask you to think of a favourite place, you can imagine what it would look, sound, feel, smell and taste like, you don't have to be seeing a picture perfect cinema version of it in your mind. You can imagine, sense, think or just know it without seeing it or picturing it in every detail.

If I asked you to imagine the sound your feet make when you walk across gravel, you know the sound I am talking about and you can imagine it. You're not necessarily hearing it physically in your ears, but you can imagine it, can't you? That is all I ask.

So, hypnosis is not like being unconscious, it is almost like having heightened awareness. It requires you to want the change, have an open, positive mind, as best as you can; and allow whatever happens to happen, without trying to grasp at what you think should happen. Just let it happen and look forward to seemingly inexplicable golf improvement and enjoyment.

Appendix 2

History of Hypnosis and NLP

The Distant Past

Hypnotism as a health aid probably originated with the Hindus of India and they mention hypnotic procedures in the Hindu Vedas written around 1500 BC. Historians believe that they operated sleep temples, like the ancient Greeks and Egyptians around 500 BC, where they gave hypnotic-like inductions and suggestions to sick people to utilise a sleep-like state. In China, Wong Tai wrote about the medical use of incantations and hand passes, around 2600 BC.

There is also evidence that people practiced hypnosis in some form more widely across the Europe and Asia in theses times. There are also earlier cave paintings suggesting trance-like practices taking place at least 6,000 years ago.

The Middle Ages

Modern science evolved rapidly between the 9th and 14th centuries across the Mediterranean. This also led to a revival of the medical and philosophical knowledge from Ancient Greece, Egypt and early Eastern civilisations. This included their development of a deeper understanding of psychology and the early precursors of the use of analysis, altered states of consciousness and hypnosis to alleviate emotional sufferings.

Pietro d'Abano, a teacher of medicine, philosophy and astrology in Padua, wrote around 1250 AD that suggestion had definite effects on some mentally disturbed people. The Inquisition twice brought him to trial for these practices, but they only found him guilty after his death.

In the early 16th Century, Paracelsus, a Swiss alchemist and physician, travelled widely in Europe, Africa and Asia learning about local medical practices, before developing the use of magnets in healing. He claimed that magnetic treatment was useful "in all inflammations, influxes, and ulcerations, in diseases of the uterus and bowels, in internal as well as external diseases. Any diseased part of the body, when exposed to a magnetic force, will be cured better and more speedily than by any medicine".

People like Valentine Greatrakes continued the use of magnets in healing sporadically over the next two centuries. In the 17th century Greatrakes was renowned as the Great Irish Stroker for his ability to heal people by laying his hands on them and passing magnets over their bodies.

The Mind-body Connection

Many traditional healers believed that the body, thoughts and emotions can influence one another. The Romans described it as *"mens sana in corpore sano"* or healthy mind in healthy body. But in the mid 18th century, the scientific developments of Newton and others lead to a separation of the treatment of the mind and body. The church reluctantly allowed the development of science in medicine, but retained control of the mind and spirit.

Dr Franz Anton Mesmer

In the late 18th century, Father Maximilian Hell, a Jesuit Priest from Vienna, used magnets to heal by applying steel plates to the naked body. He was also a well known astronomer and is renowned for his controversial observations of the transit of Venus. He also gave his name to Hell crater on the moon.

One of Father Hell's students was a young medical doctor from Vienna named Franz Anton Mesmer, who went on to be the most influential figure in the development of hypnosis in the 18th century. Mesmer was a charismatic and at times controversial physician. He developed a method he called animal magnetism using magnets and magnetised metal frames to perform passes over the patient to remove blockages, the causes of diseases, in the body's magnetic forces. He also induced a trance-like state in his patients. He found that he could produce equally successful results by the prolonged passing of his hands over the patient.

Mesmer chose the name "animal magnetism" to distinguish the force in the human body from the other magnetic forces known at the time as mineral magnetism, cosmic magnetism and planetary magnetism.

He worked in Austria, Switzerland and Germany before settling in France, where, despite his many successes the medical authorities soon derided and ostracised him, even with his support from the French king.

Mesmer's name lives on in the word "mesmerise" – to hold someone's attention to the exclusion of anything else, so as to create a trance state, in other words to hypnotise.

Armand de Puységur was a student of Mesmer and continued to develop Mesmer's work after the latter's death in 1815. He discovered that spoken words and direct commands could easily induce trance and do so noticeably faster. He called this deep trance state somnambulism and described the key characteristics as

- a concentration of the patient's senses on the therapist
- the acceptance of suggestion from the therapist
- amnesia of the events that happened in trance.

He also found that doctors could perform painless operations on patients in trance. Doctors in France developed this with Dr Recamier performing the first recorded operation in this way in 1821. In England, Dr Elliotson, Dr "Painless" Parker, who used the techniques in dentistry, and Dr James Esdaile developed this further.

Esdaile performed his first operation without anaesthetic in India and went on to perform more than 300 major operations and over a thousand minor ones using mesmerism. His results were very impressive with a mortality rate of only 5% compared to the 50% rate for other surgeons performing similar operations without hypnosis or anaesthetic.

Battlefield surgeons in the American Civil War later used hypnosis extensively for battlefield surgery. The discovery of chloroform and its use as an anaesthetic largely ended the use of hypnosis in surgery. It was much faster and required less skill for the surgeon to inject a patient than to induce hypnosis.

Abbé Faria, an Indo-Portuguese priest came from India in 1814 and revived interest for animal magnetism in Paris. Unlike Mesmer, he claimed that the power of expectancy and cooperation of the patient generated the effect in the mind – in effect, autosuggestion. This later influenced Hippolyte Bernheim and Ambroise-Auguste Liébeault of the Nancy School and subsequently the techniques of Émile Coué a hundred years later.

James Braid and Hypnotism

James Braid in the early 19th Century was the pioneer of hypnosis in Britain and introduced the term hypnosis – derived from the Greek word for sleep. He initially called it neuro-hypnosis and then changed it to hypnosis, believing that sleep was involved. When he later found that it was not actual sleep, he chose monoideaism, but hypnosis became the popular term.

A Scottish eye surgeon and optometrist, Braid probably developed an interest in mesmerism by chance when he noticed a patient in his waiting room staring with glazed eyes at a lamp. Braid told him to close his eyes and go to sleep. Others say that he first witnessed hypnotism at a demonstration of animal magnetism and was not impressed; believing it to be trickery. A second demonstration convinced him when he was able to painlessly push a pin beneath a finger-nail of a mesmerised girl.

Whichever story we believe, he discovered that getting a patient to fixate upon something, such as a swinging watch, was a way of getting them into a trance. He described this as *"protracted ocular fixation"* that fatigued certain parts of the brain and caused the "nervous sleep" – what we now call trance. Braid wrote *Neurypnology,* the first book on hypnosis, in 1843.

The Nancy and Paris Schools

Two competing schools of hypnosis started up in France in the late 19th Century and both advanced the development of hypnosis significantly. In Paris, Dr Jean-Martin Charcot, a neurologist, said that hypnosis resulted only from physical or neurological stimulation. In Nancy, Dr Ambroise-Auguste Liébeault and Dr Hippolyte Bernheim held that hypnosis is a natural state available to everyone using free will – the modern day view.

Charcot endorsed hypnotism for the treatment of hysteria using his "numerical method" and led the way with the move of hypnosis from the medical doctor to the mental health profession. They first described the process of post-hypnotic suggestion in this period and great successes including major improvements in sensory acuity and memory using hypnosis. Pierre Janet, a protégé of Charcot, introduced the idea of dissociation to aid the access of skills and memory under hypnosis. This developed interest in the subconscious and eventually to reintegration therapy for dissociated personalities.

Liébeault, a physician, first described the need for cooperation between the hypnotizer and the participant – rapport in our terms. He delivered a sequence of suggestions, in a monotonous but penetrating voice, about the patient's health, digestion, circulation, coughing and many other aspects.

Despite initial scepticism, Bernheim, a French neurologist, joined Liébeault and helped to emphasise the importance of suggestibility. Together they treated over 30,000 using hypnosis. Albert Moll, an active promoter of hypnotism in Germany around the turn of the 20th century, studied at Nancy and, with Sigmund Freud, witnessed some of Bernheim's experiments there.

Emile Coué and the Laws of Suggestion

Émile Coué, a French psychologist and pharmacist, introduced a method of healing and self-improvement based on optimistic conscious autosuggestion. He based his Coué method on the routine repetition of ritual autosuggestions, such as *"every day, in every way, I'm getting better and better"* at the beginning and the end of every day.

Coué defined the Laws of suggestion as the Law of

- Concentrated Attention – Whenever attention is concentrated on an idea over and over again, it spontaneously tends to realize itself
- Reversed Effect – The harder one tries to do something, the less chance one has of success.
- Dominant Effect – A strong emotion/suggestion tends to replace a weaker one.

Coué believed that he did not heal people, but rather facilitated their own self-healing. This concept of self-participation was the modern hypnotists' maxim "there is no such thing as hypnosis, only self-hypnosis." He also believed that imagination is more powerful than will. Walking across a plank on the floor seems much easier than walking on the same plank suspended between two tall buildings. He also anticipated modern research on the placebo effect – drugs are not always necessary for recovery from illness, but belief in recovery is.

Hypnosis in the 20th Century

Around the beginning of the 20th century, Sigmund Freud also studied under Charcot and Bernheim. He later discovered abreaction therapy using hypnosis with Josef Breuer back in Austria. Freud also made use of hypnosis in his early work, but he seems to have lost patience with it – probably because he was not a good hypnotist.

Freud's abandonment of hypnosis prejudiced its wider use in psychiatry until the second half of the 20th century. For the most part, stage hypnotists like Ormond McGill kept it alive. Despite this, doctors used hypnosis treat neuroses during World War I, World War II and the Korean War. They found that the merger of hypnosis techniques with psychiatry especially useful in the treatment of what we know today as Post Traumatic Stress Disorder.

History of Hypnosis and NLP

Many people consider that Clark Hull, an experimental psychologist at Yale University, began the modern study of hypnotism. His rigorous study of the phenomenon, using statistical and experimental analysis that he describes in his book *Hypnosis and Suggestibility*, confirmed that hypnosis is not sleep. He rubbished many of the more extreme claims for hypnosis, but proved hypnotic anaesthesia, post-hypnotic amnesia and some of the physical possibilities for hypnosis.

After World War II, medical and psychiatric interest in hypnosis rose rapidly. Ernest Hilgard, together with Josephine Hilgard and Andre Weitzenhoffer, founded a laboratory for hypnosis research at Stanford University. Hilgard's status as one of the world's most distinguished psychologists helped establish hypnosis as a legitimate subject of scientific inquiry.

Dr. Weitzenhoffer was one of the most eminent scholars of hypnosis in the 20th century. His first paper, *The Production of Anti-Social Acts Under Hypnosis* in 1949 was the first of more than 100 eventual journal publications, books, and papers on the topic of hypnosis. He also worked with Ernest Hilgard in developing the Stanford Hypnotic Susceptibility Scales and the Stanford Profile Scales of Hypnotic Susceptibility, the most widely used measures of individual differences in hypnotic responsivity.

Harry Arons, a professional hypnotist, wrote Hypnosis in Criminal Investigation in 1967 about the use of hypnosis in the judicial system. The book included such applications such as memory recall, age regression, induction techniques and confabulation. Arons also travelled the country training law enforcement agencies. His helped create national acceptance for hypnosis in the US legal community. He produced the Arons scale for the depth of trance in hypnosis – ranging from Hypnoidal to Profound Somnambulism.

Dave Elman pioneered the modern medical use of hypnosis, especially for pain release and for treating the emotional components of allergies, stuttering and obesity. Although he had no formal medical training, he trained a considerable number of physicians and psychotherapists in America, in the use of hypnotism. He encountered hypnotism as a small boy when a stage hypnotist helped his terminally ill father with pain relief.

His book *Hypnotherapy*, published in 1964, is still one of the most important hypnosis reference books and Elman is especially remembered for introducing rapid inductions to the field of hypnotism. One eponymous method of induction which he introduced more than fifty years ago is still one of the favourite inductions used today.

Milton H. Erickson

Probably the most important contributor to hypnosis in the 20th century and to the acceptance of hypnotherapy, as both art and science, was the grandfather of hypnotherapy – Dr Milton H. Erikson. Dr Erikson was a psychiatrist and hypnotherapist with outstanding professional credentials and because of his solid medical background he had credibility within the medical profession.

Erickson was also hugely influential in the development of NLP by Richard Bandler and John Grinder. Along with Fritz Perls and Virginia Satir, he was one of the key people Bandler and Grinder chose to model when they started out.

Neuro Linguistic Programming – NLP

Before looking at the history of NLP, it's important to answer the question – what exactly is NLP? There are many answers, recipes and incantations in books written by a host of authors. The best answer comes from Richard Bandler, the co-developer of NLP with John Grinder. Taking a deep breath,

"NLP is an attitude... characterised by a sense of curiosity and adventure and a desire to learn the skills to be able to find out what kinds of communication influences somebody and the kinds of things worth knowing; to look at life as a rare and unprecedented opportunity to learn.

NLP is a methodology... based on the overall operational presupposition that all behaviour has a structure and that structure can be modelled, learned, taught and changed (re-

programmed). The way to know what will be useful and effective are the perceptual skills.

NLP has evolved as an innovative technology... enabling the practitioner to organise information and perceptions in ways that allow them to achieve results that were once inconceivable."

The Presuppositions of NLP are another way of looking at it, as

1. the map is not the territory
2. there is no failure only feedback
3. mind and body are part of the same system
4. everyone is doing the best they can with the resources available to them
5. if it is possible for someone, it is possible for me
6. the system (person) with the most flexibility of behaviour will have the most influence on the system
7. the meaning of communication is the response it produces
8. you're in charge of your mind and therefore your results
9. all the resources we need are inherent to our own physiology.

Richard Bandler and John Grinder initially developed NLP (Neuro-linguistic Programming) out of a behavioural modelling project they ran in the early 1970's at the University of California in Santa Cruz, 70 miles south of San Francisco. Bandler was studying philosophy, logic, computer science and mathematics and teaching Gestalt Therapy at the same time. Grinder was soon to become a professor of linguistics.

The link to hypnosis came from the advice of Gregory Bateson, Bandler's landlord, mentor and a renowned British anthropologist, social scientist, linguist, and cyberneticist. He advised Bandler to model Milton Erickson, as we have already heard, the foremost clinical hypnotherapist of the 20th century. Bandler and Grinder were already modelling Fritz Perls the creator of Gestalt Therapy and Virginia Satir, a well known psychologist specialising in family therapy.

As the NLP movement grew, they tested their ideas and techniques on their friends and any student they could lay their hands on. The team soon expanded to include others including

Robert Dilts, Judith DeLozier, Leslie Cameron, soon to become Leslie Cameron Bandler, Terry McLendon and David Gordon.

They soon developed many the techniques we know today, including anchoring, sensory acuity and calibration, reframing, representational systems, and the two Language Models – the Meta Model and the Milton Model. They also developed many other personal change techniques.

The pioneers of NLP documented these techniques in a prolific series of books through the 70's and early 80's, starting with the Structure of Magic volumes I and II and Patterns of the Hypnotic Techniques of Milton H. Erickson, MD Volume 1 and Volume 2. They published all of these in the first 5 years and then supplemented them with a series of transcripts of seminars conducted by Bandler and Grinder. The best known and most influential of these was Frogs into Princes published in 1979.

The NLP bandwagon continued apace during the 80's and 90's despite the original creators Bandler and Grinder breaking up, with the ensuing legal battles. Regardless of this, NLP continues to grow and develop with Bandler and Grinder still leading the two main factions, closely followed by the Tony Robbins camp and others. The factionalism also exists in the NLP "standards" bodies that have evolved, probably still led by Bandler's Society of NLP (SNLP).

We are fortunate to have a broad spectrum on NLP trainers in the UK including Richard Bandler, who has teamed up Paul McKenna, the famous stage hypnotist, to deliver regular NLP courses in the UK. Richard also teaches NLP elsewhere in the world, often teaming up with the President of the SNLP, John La Valle and many others.

John Grinder has teamed up with Carmen Bostic St Clair and Michael Carroll to promote and train his New Code NLP in the UK.

Official Recognition or Hypnosis

Theologians, religious leaders and medical authorities have long expressed concern that, if not applied properly, hypnosis could deprive a person of their faculty of reason. Saint Thomas Aquinas rebuts this from the grave in his words *"The loss of reason is not a sin in itself but only by reason of the act by which one is deprived of the use of reason. If the act that deprives one of his uses of reason is licit in itself and is done for a just cause, there is no sin; if no just cause is present, it must be considered a venial sin"*.

The Catholic Church seemed to have forgotten this by the time of the Inquisition, as Pietro d'Abano found out. However, on July 28, 1847, the Roman Curia issued a decree stating that *"Having removed all misconception, foretelling of the future, explicit or implicit invocation of the devil, the use of animal magnetism (Hypnotism) is indeed merely an act of making use of physical media that are otherwise licit and hence it is not morally forbidden provided it does not tend toward an illicit end or toward anything depraved"*. Pope Pius XII further endorsed this in 1956 when he stated, in his address from the Vatican on hypnosis in childbirth, that the use of hypnosis by health care professionals for diagnosis and treatment is permitted.

The British Medical Association (BMA) drafted a resolution in 1891 in favour of the use of hypnosis in medicine, but did not approve it until 1955. That was 64 years later and 3 years after the introduction of the British Hypnotism Act in 1952. The Act regulates the public demonstration of stage hypnotists for entertainment.

The BMA resolution approved the use of hypnosis in the areas of psychoneuroses and hypnoanesthesia for pain management in childbirth and surgery. The BMA now advises all physicians and medical students to receive fundamental training in hypnosis.

Skills for Health, the Government's Sector Skills Council for the UK health industry published National Occupational Standards (NOS) for Hypnotherapy in 2002.

In the US, the American Medical Association approved a report on the medical uses of hypnosis in 1958 and encouraged research on hypnosis. However, it did point out that some aspects of hypnosis are unknown and controversial.

Two years after AMA approval, the American Psychological Association endorsed hypnosis as a branch of psychology.

Appendix 3

"Your Own Virtual Caddy" Transcript

Welcome to this "your own virtual caddy" hypnosis experience with me Andrew Fogg – The Golf Hypnotist. Please ensure that you're seated in a comfortable position, so that you can relax and be most comfortable.

If at any time you wish to emerge from hypnosis before the session comes to an end, all you need to do is to count from 1 to 5 and open your eyes. You can count either out loud or to yourself and every time on 5... you're completely emerged from hypnosis.

Make yourself comfortable now or as soon as you're ready... Now... and I don't know now if you will have both feet flat on the ground... or on the footrest of the chair... while your hands are just separate... hands... apart right and left... and right on your legs... or perhaps the arms of your chair... Aren't they... whatever is right for you... And I don't know if you've noticed that it's better to have your feet apart... or your legs left uncrossed... while you're sitting right there on the chair.

And you may be thinking consciously about what I am... saying... these words to you... While the more you listen... to me... the less you're understanding... with your conscious mind... Aren't you... Because it's your ears that I am speaking to... And your conscious mind can only be aware of so much... while your unconscious mind knows... everything you know... now don't you... So it doesn't matter... if one of you feels the need to move slightly... now and again... Does it... As you don't have to be absolutely still... while you're feeling comfortable... or just sitting there... Now... Aren't you...

And, I don't know if you want to take a deep breath in now...or now in a minute...before holding it for a moment...and then just releasing it slowly... That's good...to breathe just as slowly....deeply...and comfortably as you need...now...you're deeply comfortable...I don't know if your eyes are already closed... now or if they will just flicker...and close now... or as you remain in full control...responding hypnotically...only to my intended suggestions...as you're fully protected from random thought, random image and random sound becoming hypnotic suggestion.

And as you've been sitting there... paying attention to what we have been saying... and as each word reaches you... know that my voice will go with you...as you can begin to realise... that you're already learning about many things... which have already begun... to help you to transform... Your unconscious... knows that there are many changes... that you've been looking for... Here and now... you can notice that... as you begin to think of... what you want... you'll find yourself seeing it positively... specifically. You'll imagine what you will be able to see... hear and feel... when you've achieved it... You'll imagine what will happen... as a result... and what part of all of it... is under your control.

While your unconscious...has recorded everything...all of your experiences...and in the database of your unconscious...Now....everything you've ever seen...now...everything you ever heard...now...everything you've ever felt, smelt, taste it...now...and everything you've ever said to yourself...now...it's stored...Now...in your unconscious mind...So, consciously... you may be wandering...how you can change this...because it is your unconscious mind...that knows how to change...and to do it in a in a timely and easy way...Whether or not you consciously think you know what to do...it's your unconscious...mind...that can begin considering...what it is that's really important to you...can it not.

And you relax even deeper... you'll enjoy the wonderful feeling... that comes with letting go... you'll become fascinated with the different perceptions... you experience which move... change and evolve... and you can find yourself... letting every

"Your Own Virtual Caddy" Transcript

part of your body and mind... relax... as you allow yourself to make certain changes... and changes in certainty... you can let go of the beliefs about golf... which you had and understand about golf... is simply about learning that... you can feel this comfortable... wonderful state of inner peace... and from here you can allow yourself to experience wonderful confident and happy feelings... which seep inside your skin... helping you feel really good... and finding yourself... easily and completely... to change the way you felt... to all those things which did produce average golf.

Now, in their place... you're finding yourself... feeling only good feelings...

feelings which inspire you... feelings which motivate you... into realising how you can see things... in an entirely new way... you can find yourself learning to see the same experience... from another point of view and develop... inside your mind... an enjoyable way of thinking about everything... so that in the future... as you play golf... in your unconscious... mind you... will find yourself seeing them in many different ways... from many different perspectives... with a wonderful sense of happiness... which helps you enjoy everything... effortlessly.

You'll enjoy the wonderful moment... that allows you to understand your golf differently... and inspires you to take the action... that is necessary to turn your golfing life around. You've learned many things... which you will find you can... use dramatically... to enhance your golf... and as you use all these skills... you'll become delightfully surprised... with how quick and easy... permanent... positive these changes are for you.

Now... This is your own virtual caddy programme... and every time you're about to play golf... You feel confident... enthusiastic... calm... positive... and happy... as you really look forward... to your game of golf... and every time you think about playing golf... and plan your next round... you know that the pleasure of golf is in competing... with the golf course... isn't it. As the other players... your partners... your opponents and golfing companions... are competing... and it doesn't matter... they are just other people playing the golf course... now... your own virtual caddy starts to work for you... before you start out on the round... perhaps while you're on your way to the course or perhaps when you arrive at the club... then... you think about the round of golf you're about to play... you consider the nature of the course... you're playing so well on... and you also think about all those good shots you've played in your golfing life... and all those better and better shots you're going to play... now... and in the future... You've planned how you're going to play this round of golf... and I don't know if you have the opportunity to practise before the round... or just to warm up with a few free swings... as you remember how much better you're playing... now... your inner caddy reminds you how good your swing looks today... before... you're taking some time to warm up on the putting green... just loosening up and increasing your putting confidence... and it doesn't matter if you hole the practice putts...as you learn the feel of the greens...now...today... while your inner caddy comments on how good the greens are today for you...and how well you're putting.

And when you're prepared, you feel a fascinating sense of absolute calmness... confidence...and enthusiasm and relaxed expectation... as you both realise how well you can play... now...today... and this round... is about to begin...as you arrive on your first tee...again feeling calm and confident...as you know you have your own caddy who really understands you... your inner caddy... there to help you every step of the way and every shot and putt of the round.

And every time you arrive at your ball or step onto the teeing ground... your inner caddy is there with you... ready to advise and guide you... and that gives you even more confidence as you just know that you're going to enjoy playing well today... full of confidence... and calmness... and enthusiasm... and optimism... Now... as your inner caddy reminds you... concentrate...and focus on to the shot you're about to play...well... as you imagine... you jointly assess the shot or putt you're about to play... your inner caddy coaches you through your pre-shot routine... talking over the shot that are about to play... taking into consideration the lie... the nature of the ground... whether it's uphill... or downhill... or sidehill or flat... as you think about the target area... where you

"Your Own Virtual Caddy" Transcript

want to land the ball... the precise spot...as you and your caddie decide where to land the ball ...considering the wind...the temperature...the slopes... the safe side of the hole...and you both consider your capabilities... as your inner caddie reminds you of good shots... you've hit... like this one... now... well... within your capabilities... so you have more and more confidence that you can do it... together... now... just as soon as you're ready... your inner caddy reminds you to step back and visualise yourself playing that shot perfectly... watching the ball travel to your chosen target... in just the way you both imagine... it's happening now... and your caddy reminds you to make a rehearsal swing... just turning that visualisation into reality...and just as soon as you complete a perfect rehearsal stroke... I don't know it will be the first stroke or the second... and the second you're confidently swinging... your inner caddie reminds you to take a deep relaxing breath... and let go both your conscious awareness... as you step in and take your stance... your unconscious... knows what to do... and you unconsciously make your best ... most natural... most relaxed and most experienced stroke at the ball... now... every time... better and better.

And every time you see the shot flying and the putt rolling... you know... that you have done the best you can... better and better every time perhaps... as you watch the result... you gain new learnings... leading you to better and better shots...as your inner caddy reminds you... and you know... now... that whatever the result... you have both done your best... as you release the shot to history... and consciously relax your focus and concentration... ready for the time to when you're ready for your next shot.

And as you move along happily to your next shot... your caddy reminds you to relax and take in the scenery... looking up... things are always looking up... more and more... as you see the sky... the clouds, perhaps... the birds... as you enjoy this wonderful experience of playing golf... sometimes exchanging pleasantries with your playing companions... recharging your batteries...as you relax more and more between shots... ready for your inner caddy to remind you to concentrate on the next shot... every time... better and better... now and through to the completion of each hole... and the end of the round.

And at the end of every round...your inner caddy reminds you to remember... every time... to recall the best three shots... you played... as your inner caddy stores them in the very depths of your unconscious... building and growing your database of great shots that you can hit whenever you want... memorising memories of how increasingly better you play and enjoy golf... every time you play... now... and in the future.

And this increasing knowledge... gives you confidence... more and more... so that when you sleep... at night after playing golf... and at other times... your sleep is better and better... and increasingly more relaxed... and when... perhaps...you dream of increasingly better and more enjoyable golf... and your dreams are a wonderful embodiment... of the great new feelings that you have about golf...so that when you wake up... you feel revitalised... full of increasing energy and relaxed confidence.

And that relaxed confidence means that every time you enter hypnosis... with a hypnotist... using self-hypnosis... or listening to hypnotic recordings... now... your hypnosis is deeper and deeper and increasingly more effective... so that... each time suggestions have more and more beneficial effect upon you...consequently whenever you think about golf... you feel an unexplained sense of anticipation... and just know that every time you play golf... you're getting better and better... and gaining increasing enjoyment... fulfilment... and pleasure from your golf.

Now... just imagine preparing for and playing your next round of golf... I don't know whether it will be in the next few days... in the next few weeks... or just some time in the future... and take a few moments... now... to think about that experience... how much more relaxed... confident... enthusiastic... and optimistic... you're feeling... as you move out onto the course... playing that round... knowing... you're in company with your inner caddy... reminding you of the important things... to remember... when you need to remember them... because your inner caddy helps you... more and more every time you play.

And now... in a moment... but not yet... not until you're ready... but in a moment... thank your unconscious mind... and you inner caddy... for these wonderful learnings... this pleasant

"Your Own Virtual Caddy" Transcript

relaxing experience... as they store your own virtual caddy program into the deepest recesses of your unconscious... ready and prepared for your increasing future enjoyment of golf and your rapidly improving golfing ability.

And in a moment... I will count you up from one... to five... and out of hypnosis... but not just yet.

So, when I say one... you will have full control, flexibility and coordination throughout your whole body... from the tips of your toes... to the top of your head... from the tips of your fingers and thumbs... to your shoulders... any feelings of lightness... and/or heaviness... return to there to their true and correct perspective

When I say two... you will position yourself back in the place you now are... remembering and recalling... what is to your left and right... above and below... remembering and recalling some features of this place.

At three... all sounds will be back in their correct perspective... and have their true levels of importance.

At four... you will bring back with you this present... to the present... and to the future... your own virtual caddy... always available to you whenever you play golf... Now.

Five... you will open your eyes to emerge fully... from this hypnosis session... and feeling really wonderful... relaxed... fresh... clean... and confident... ready to achieve your full potential as a golfer.

And as I count you up from 1 to 5... one... two... three... four...and five... open you eyes... and take a deep breath in and relax.

About the Author

Andrew Fogg, The Golf Hypnotist has been a fanatical golfer for the last 40 years! And his purpose in life is to help you achieve your full potential as a golfer. That means playing beyond the limits of your physical capability by putting your golf mind effectively to work. He's not saying that the golf swing and physical technique aren't important, just that those are not his specialist areas – there are thousands of very proficient professional golf teachers out there who can help you with that. His skill is in the mental side of the game and he just loves helping people. He's a golf psychologist using hypnosis and NLP in personal face-to-face sessions and he's also a practicing clinical hypnotherapist.

As a golfer, Andrew's had a helter-skelter experience with the game since taking up the golf at 18. With only a little natural talent, his first-ever handicap was 12 and by the end of that first year he was down to 4! He got hooked, as many of us golfers do, and played as often as he could and practiced when he couldn't play. He hit so many balls on the practice range at Brookmans Park Golf Club, that there was hardly any turf left on the practice tee. And probably left grooves in the practice putting green, not to mention the carpet at home.

Andrew spent a lot of time over those 40 years working on his swing, with help from a series of very good teachers. He owes a lot to Colin Christison, his first Club Pro at Brookmans Park, who taught him the basics of golf and introduced him to a lot of good golfers. He also had a few good years learning from Bill Shankland, then Pro at Potters Bar Golf Club. Colin had been the senior assistant there with Ian Connelly – later to become Nick Faldo's first coach – and of course the former junior assistant, Tony Jacklin. An early highlight of Andrew's golfing experience came when Bill invited him to take his place in a reunion game with Colin, Ian and Tony at Brookmans Park in June 1970 - when Tony was the reigning US Open Champion. That was some experience for Andrew, at the age of 20. When Bill retired, he introduced Andrew to another legend and he started having lessons from Dai Rees, the captain of the famous 1957 Ryder Cup team. There have been many more golf coaches since then!

So how did he improve with all that practice and great coaching? Well, not that much. And over those 40 years his handicap has ranged from 2 to 8, with many peaks, troughs and little consistency. That was the main reason he got interested in golf psychology and discovered his aptitude for hypnosis and NLP.

Andrew completed his NLP Practitioner training under the guidance of Richard Bandler, co-founder of NLP; Paul McKenna, the world-famous hypnotist; John La Valle, the president of the Society of NLP; and Michael Neill, the internationally renowned success coach and the best-selling author of *You Can Have What You Want* and *Feel Happy Now!* He later completed his NLP Master Practitioner and NLP Hypnosis certifications with the same team and has recently assisted on an NLP Practitioner training course with another organization.

As his interest in hypnosis developed, he qualified as a Clinical Hypnotherapist after completing the Hypnotherapy Diploma Course with Adam Eason, the world renowned hypnotherapist, trainer and best-selling author of The Secrets of Self Hypnosis, The Hypnotic Salesman and The Secrets of High Self-Esteem. He is also licensed and certified to run Adam's 2-day Self-Hypnosis Seminars.

Andrew is a family man and his wife, daughter and two wonderful granddaughters are his number one priority. After them, comes his golf and his work as a golf psychologist – it's what he loves doing, so it's not really work.

He currently lives in the Royal County of Berkshire with a wonderful array of fantastic traditional golf courses on his doorstep, including The Berkshire, Wentworth, and Sunningdale. He's a member locally at Mill Ride and, despite moving 20 miles away a couple of years ago, he's still a member after 30 years at Beaconsfield Golf Club, a traditional Harry Colt Designed course in Buckinghamshire.

About the Author

If you're interested in Andrew's golf articles, video clips, what's happening in sports psychology, news from the world of Hypnosis, Self Hypnosis and Neuro Linguistic Programming, the latest stories in the golf world and his views, reviews and commentaries on the things that interest him, then have a look at his blog page at www.golf-hypnotist.com/blog. You can also sign-up there to receive his regular free Golf-Hypnotist ezine and get a free download of his 25-minute "Your Own Virtual Caddy" golf-hypnosis audio recording that goes with Chapter 12, *Being "Your Own Virtual Caddie"*.

www.golf-hypnotist.com